The Handbook of Biblical Numismatics

45th Anniversary Edition

Mel Wacks

Coin Values by Ira Goldberg

Copyright © 2021 by Mel Wacks

Published by Mel Wacks, Woodland Hills, California

Printed in the United States of America

First Printing, 2021

Library of Congress Control Number: 2020923549

ISBN 978-0-578-81065-2

Book design provided by Lianna Spurrier under sponsorship of Newman Numismatic Portal.

The text for this book may be found online at the Newman Numismatic Portal.

*Dedicated to those who have informed and inspired me: Frederic Madden,
Rev. Edgar Rogers, Paul Romanoff Ph.D., A. Reifenberg Ph.D., Leo Kadman,
Ya'akov Meshorer, and my good friend David Hendin.*

Mel Wacks

Fellow of ANS *ANA Presidential Award* *AINA President Emeritus* *Winner of four NLG Writing Awards* *JAHF Founding Director*

Table of Contents

Introduction..6
Before there were Coins...8
The Only Coins Mentioned In The Old Testament..9
Alexander The Great In Judaea...10
The Shekel Of Tyre..12
The First Judaean Coins..15
The Syrian-Judaean Connection...17
Maccabees/Hasmoneans...19
The Last Of The Maccabees...23
The Widow's Mite...25
A Tale of Three Camels 27
"Judaea Capta" Precursor..31
Herod The Great..33
The Herodian Dynasty...36
Herod's Grandchildren..39
The Herodian Kings Of Armenia..42
The Prefects & Procurators...44
The Tribute Penny...48
The First Revolt...50
Judaea Capta..56
Nerva Reforms Jewish Tax..60
The Kitos War..62
Hadrian's Trip To Judaea...64
The Second Revolt..66
City Coins of Palestine..72
Scenes from the Bible..76
Islamic Coins Inspired by Ancient Judaean Coins..79
Israel Coins Inspired by Ancient Judaean Coins..81
About the Author...85
Appendix A   Ancient Hebrew Coin Inscriptions..86
Appendix B   The Holy Of Holies on Ancient Judaean Coins...............................91
Appendix C   Roman Tenth Legion Counterstamps..96
Appendix D   About Ira Goldberg...98
Appendix E   Estimated Coin Values by Ira Goldberg...101
Appendix F   False Shekels...102
Appendix G   Enlarged Photos of Small Coins..104
Appendix H   Poppies or Pomegranates?...112
Index...115
Photo Credits...117

Introduction

I strongly believe that there is no collecting thrill that surpasses holding a genuine 2,000 year old Judaean or a related coin in your hands. Who held it before you? The High Priest at the Temple in Jerusalem? Shimon Bar Kochba, leader of the Second Revolt who was proclaimed to be the Messiah by the renowned Rabbi Akiva? Jesus? The historian Josephus? The thought boggles the mind.

You can't touch these coins at the Israel Museum in Jerusalem, or the British Museum in London — but you can actually own them, for a cost starting at under $100! Also included, is a Jewish Shekel that has sold for over a million dollars! I have written this Handbook as a starting guide to help you pick a few coins that you would like to own, or to assemble a comprehensive collection.

Reading about "Bible coins" is fun — owning one or more is fantastic. Here are my suggestions on how to collect these coins:

(1) You can buy in person at a dealer or coin show, or at auction, or on the Internet. Buying face-to-face with a dealer allows you to carefully examine coins, compare one to the other, and get valuable information from the dealer. Unfortunately, there are few dealers specializing in these coins in the United States; but if you are ever fortunate enough to visit Israel, there are numerous dealers there. It is important that you find a reputable dealer — who preferably is a member of the American Numismatic Association, American Numismatic Society, International Association of Professional Numismatists, etc. — such as the companies listed in Photo Credits at the end of this book. I do not recommend buying ancient coins from dealers who do not specialize in this kind of material, or on those selling on ebay or elsewhere on the Internet.

(2) Buy the best quality that you can comfortably afford. I suggest seeking out bronze coins in at least Fine to Very Fine condition; Extremely Fine if possible. For silver coins, I recommend buying at least Very Fine examples; preferably Extremely Fine or better. Buying well worn coins of any kind will rarely be rewarding; you will not have pride of ownership and they are difficult to sell.

(3) You will have to decide whether to collect slabbed/certified coins. On one hand, you can be sure that these are genuine and graded properly. But, on the other hand, you lose the thrill of holding the coin in your hand. That's a personal decision. I have no slabbed ancient coins in my collection, but I am old fashioned.

(4) Half the fun is in research. I suggest you read as much as possible. It really is not that

Fig. 1
Year 2 Shekel "slabbed" by NGC vs. "raw" coin.

6 The Handbook of Biblical Numismatics

difficult to learn how to read the coin inscriptions in ancient Hebrew/Aramaic (see Appendix A). Some of the ancient Hebrew letters actually look a lot like the English alphabet. You can learn more about these ancient coins on the Internet, such as the free resources on the Newman Numismatic Portal (nnp.wustl.edu/library/periodicals) — *The Shekel* magazine, published by the American Israel Numismatic Association (1968-present), and *The Augur*, published by the Biblical Numismatic Society (1977-1983). If you want to dig further, I strongly suggest that you obtain a copy of David Hendin's *Guide to Biblical Coins* on www.amazon.com or elsewhere. Please note that the H-number in each picture caption of this book refers to the 5th edition of Hendin's comprehensive standard reference.

I use the terms BCE (Before the Common Era) and CE (Common Era) as opposed to BC and AD. The term "Common Era" can be found in English as early as 1708 (*The History of the Works of the Learned*); in the later 20th century, the use of CE and BCE was popularized in academic and scientific publications as culturally neutral terms.

I hope that you will have as much fun and satisfaction from reading the 45th Anniversary edition of *The Handbook of Biblical Numismatics* as I have had in writing it.

Mel

Before there were Coins

There are a multitude of references to values of exchange in the Bible — shekels, bekas, talents, etc. Around 2000 BCE, when Abraham's servant first saw Rebekah, the future wife of Isaac, he "**took a golden earring of half a shekel weight, and two bracelets for her hands of ten shekels weight of gold**" (*Genesis 24:22*). There were no coins at this time, so about a half ounce of silver was weighed as the equivalent of a shekel.

In the early 13th century BCE, "**The Lord spake unto Moses, saying ... Every one that passeth among them that are numbered, (males) from twenty years old and above, shall give an offering unto the Lord ... half a shekel after the shekel of the sanctuary (a shekel is twenty gerahs)**" (*Exodus 30:13*). A crude piece of silver, now called "Hacksilber," that could have been used at that time, is pictured

Fig. 2
Right: Half Shekel, silver "Hacksilber," c. 13th-10th century BCE, 5.4 grams. Courtesy of Dr. Robert Deutsch, ex Prof. Ehud Malberger collection. Left: Hoard of silver "Hacksilber" ingots, late 8-7th century BCE.

By 800 BCE, there was a rather sophisticated system of weights established, based on the shekel. Standard weights were polished domed stones, engraved with the weight — from fractions to multiples of a shekel.

Fig. 3
A selection of Judaean Stone Weights, L to R: 8 Gerah (3.96gm), Beqa (6.7gm), Pym (8.8gm), Shekel (10.7gm), and 8 Shekels (90gm).

The Only Coins Mentioned in the Old Testament

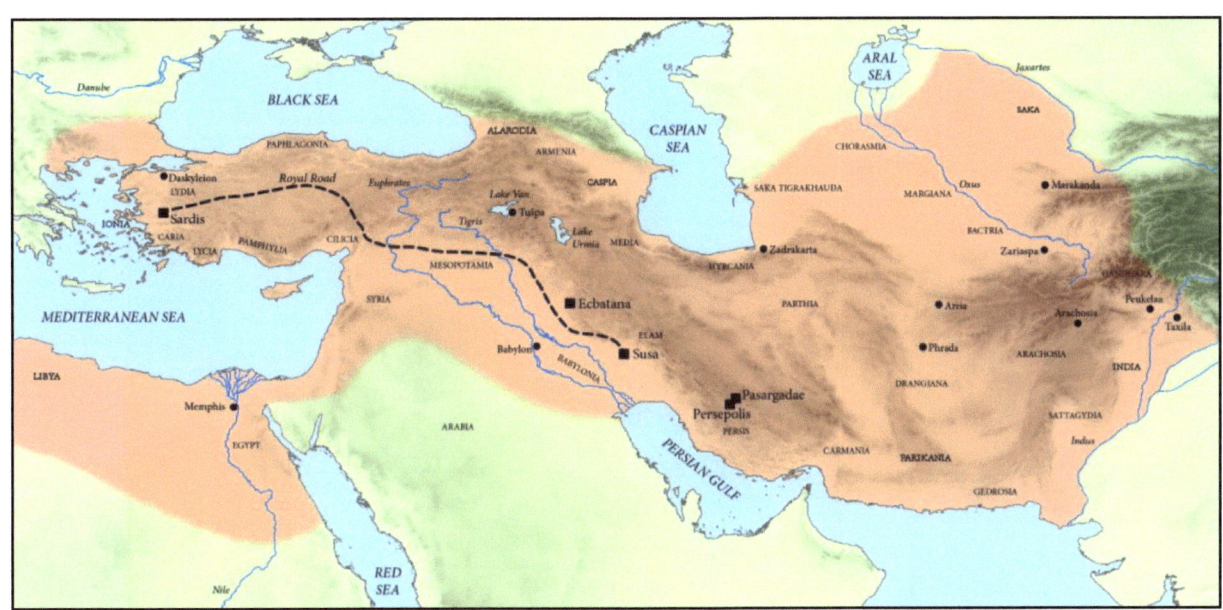

Fig. 4
Map of the Persian Kingdom, c. 500 BCE. Courtesy of the Oxford Atlas of World History (2002).

After the Greeks invented coins (c. 8th century BCE) it took a few hundred years for this vital commercial development to result in the issuance of coins in or near Judaea.

The earliest coins to depict a real person, rather than a mythological figure, were also the first and only coins referred to in the Old Testament.

The Persian gold darics (named for King Darius) were issued almost unchanged in design from c. 521-330 BCE. The Persian king — Darius, Xerxes or Artaxerxes — is shown running with a spear, sword and/or bow and arrow. *Ezra 2:1 & 69* indicates that: "And these are the people of the province who went up from the captivity of the exile, whom Nebuchadnezzar, the king of Babylon, had exiled to Babylon, and they returned to Jerusalem and Judea, each one to his city ... According to their ability, they gave to the treasury of the work [to rebuild the Temple]; gold [darics?], sixty-one thousand drachmas [sigloi?] …"

#1
Persian Daric c. 420-375 BCE (H-Fig. 4.1).

Similar silver siglos coins likely formed the "ten thousand talents of silver" (equal to approximately 90 million sigloi!) paid by Haman into "the king's (Ahasuerus = Artaxerxes?) treasuries" (*Esther 2:9*), so that the king would destroy the Jews.

#2
Persian Siglos, 4th century BCE (H--).

Mel Wacks 9

Alexander the Great in Judaea

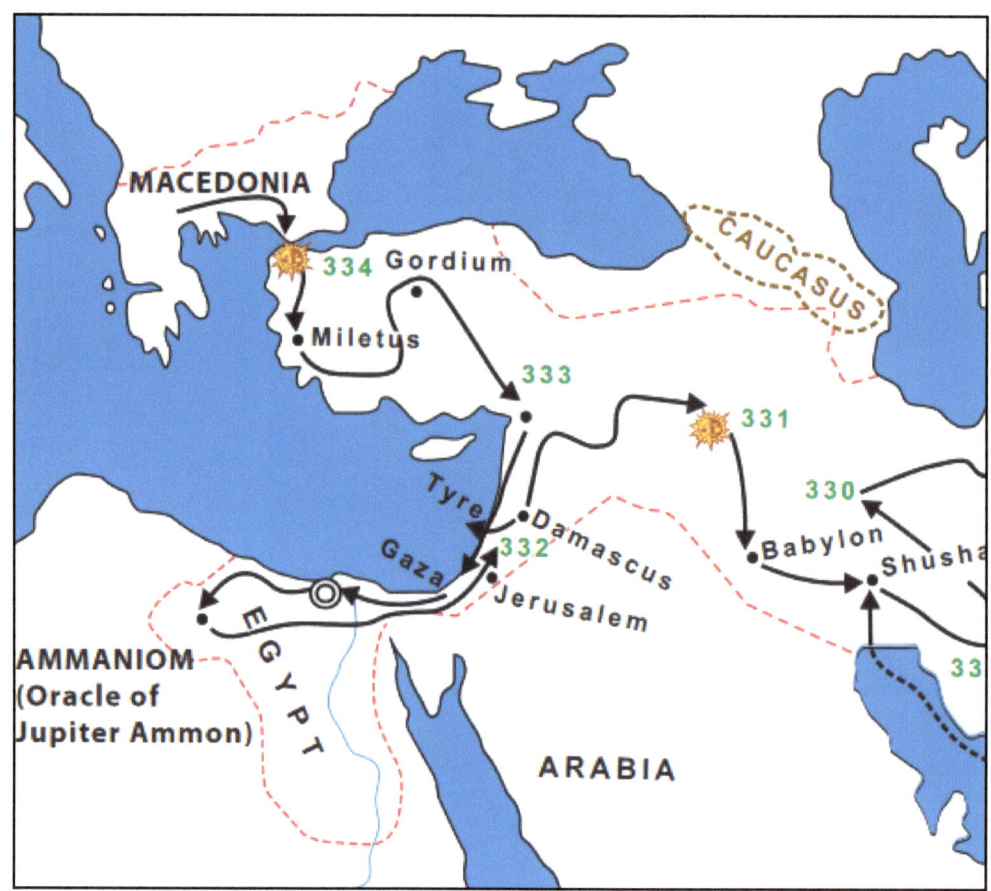

Fig. 5
Map of the Campaigns of Alexander the Great, 334-330 BCE. Courtesy of The Map Archive.

Alexander the Great set out for Persia in 334 BCE at the head of an army of 35,000. He defeated Darius III and confiscated the Persian treasury. Alexander continued south, rapidly conquering the major Phoenician cities of Aradus, Sidon and Tyre. Continuing south along the coast, Akko surrendered without a fight, and Alexander captured Gaza in 332 BCE, after a two-month siege. "And he gathered a mighty strong host and ruled over countries, and nations, and kings, who became tributaries unto him" (*Book of Maccabees I:1*).

Josephus told of Alexander's visit to the Temple in Jerusalem (translated by William Whiston): "And when he had said this to Parmenion, and had given the high-priest his right hand, the priests ran along by him, and he came into the city. And when he went up into the temple, he offered sacrifice to God, according to the high-priest's direction, and magnificently treated both the high-priest and the priests." However, "Most scholars agree that [this] story, told by the Jewish historian Flavius Josephus in his *Jewish Antiquities 11.317-345*, is not true ... the story is a bit too good to be true" (historian Jona Lendering on www.livius.org).

By the time of Alexander's untimely death at the age of 32, the youthful ruler of the civilized world had established twenty major mints from Italy to Asia — their main outputs were large silver tetradrachms, featuring a handsome portrait of the god Hercules (some say it is actually Alexander); the reverse shows the god Zeus on a throne, surrounded by the Greek inscription "King Alexander."

#3
Alexander the Great (posthumous) tetradrachm, attributed either to the Akko (Judaea) or Tyre (Phoenicia) mint, 322/1 BCE (H-1090).

Some of these tetradrachms have inscriptions in Phoenician script — the letters 'ayin and kaph and a local date. A difference of opinion among experts is summed up by Prof. Orin Tal (*The Greek Coinages of Palestine, The Oxford Handbook of Greek and Roman Coinage, 2012*): "According to A. Lemaire [*Premières monnaies avec signes cunéiformes: Samarie, IV éme s.av.n.è. Nouvelles Assyriologiques Breves et Utilitaires, 1994*], Acco did not mint coins at all during this period. Rather these coins are to be attributed to Tyre and the Phoenician letters 'ayin and kaph should be seen as abbreviating the ruler 'Azimilik [c. 349-310 BCE]. Lemair based his assumption on bronze coins in which the Greek letters TY appear alongside the Phoenician letters. However M. J. Price [*The Coinage in the Name of Alexander the Great and Philip Arrhidaeus: A British Museum Catalogue. Zurich, 1991.*] discounted Lemaire's objections and argued that this was coincidental, since Greek letters could represent a name."

So collectors can choose to think for themselves whether Alexander the Great issued coins from the Judaean mint of Akko or the Phoenician mint of Tyre.

The Shekel of Tyre

Fig. 6
Map showing the Phoenician city of Tyre in relation to cities in Judaea.

The silver shekels and half shekels issued by the Phoenician city of Tyre (c. 126 BCE - 66 CE) are perhaps the most significant of all Bible coins for both Jews and Christians. These coins, produced in large quantities, became the standard silver coinage in the Phoenician-Judaean area, replacing the coins of Alexander the Great.

The obverse features the representation of Melkart (Baal), the chief deity of the Phoenicians. The reverse shows an Egyptian-style eagle with its right claw resting on a ship's rudder (referring to Tyre's port), a club (Melkart is associated with Hercules), the Greek inscription "Tyre the Holy and Inviolable," and a date (the number of years since the acknowledgment of Tyre's independence by Syria).

#4
Shekel of Tyre, 121/120 BCE (H-1618).

The Jews had no silver coins of their own throughout the period of Tyrian shekels and half shekels. But all of the Judaean taxes were specified in shekels (e.g. the annual Temple Tax for males over 20 was specified as half a shekel): **"This they shall give, everyone who goes through the counting: half a shekel according to the holy shekel. Twenty gerahs equal one shekel; half of [such] a shekel shall be an offering to the Lord"** (*Exodus 30:13*). So the Temple Priests had to devise a practical solution. They decided that the Tyrian coins were plentiful and of good silver quality, and so they prescribed that the various Judaean taxes could be accepted only in Tyrian coins — even though they went against prohibitions of the First Commandment: **"You shall have no other gods beside Me. You shall not make for yourself a sculptured image or any likeness of what is in the heavens above, or on earth below, or in the waters under the earth"** (*Exodus 20:3*).

#5
Half shekel of Tyre, 76/5 BCE (H--).

When **"Jesus went into the temple of God, and ... overthrew the tables of the moneychangers"** (*Matthew 21:12*), he was attacking those who exchanged Tyrian coins for others, detected counterfeits, etc.

Fig. 7
Jesus overthrowing the tables of the money changers in the Temple. Engraving by Gustave Doré.

It was also, very likely, a shekel of Tyre that Jesus and Peter used to pay the Temple Tax (1/2 shekel each): *"Go thou to the sea, and cast an hook, and take up the fish that first cometh up; and when thou hast opened his mouth, thou shalt find a piece of money. That take, and give unto them for me and thee"* (*Matthew 17:27*). And finally, these coins probably made up the infamous payment to Judas, when *"they covenanted with him for thirty pieces of silver"* (*Matthew 26:15*).

#6
Shekel of Tyre, Jerusalem Mint? 33/34 CE (H-1620). This year is probably that of Jesus' execution.

Scholar Ya'akov Meshorer has written that "the shekels of Tyre on which the inscription KP appears (18 BCE - 66 CE) have in most cases, an inferior style ... and the majority have been found in Israel." He proposes that Tyre must have discontinued these coins in 19 BCE, and Jewish authorities continued minting them in Jerusalem because they were the only coins acceptable for tax payments; the series came to an end at the outbreak of the First Revolt in 66 CE.

Meshorer concludes by quoting a Jewish commentary: *"Silver, whenever mentioned in the Pentateuch, is Tyrian silver. What is a Tyrian silver (coin)? It is a Jerusalemite"* (*Tosephta Kethuboth 13:20*). However, this theory has not been unanimously accepted by experts.

The First Judaean Coins

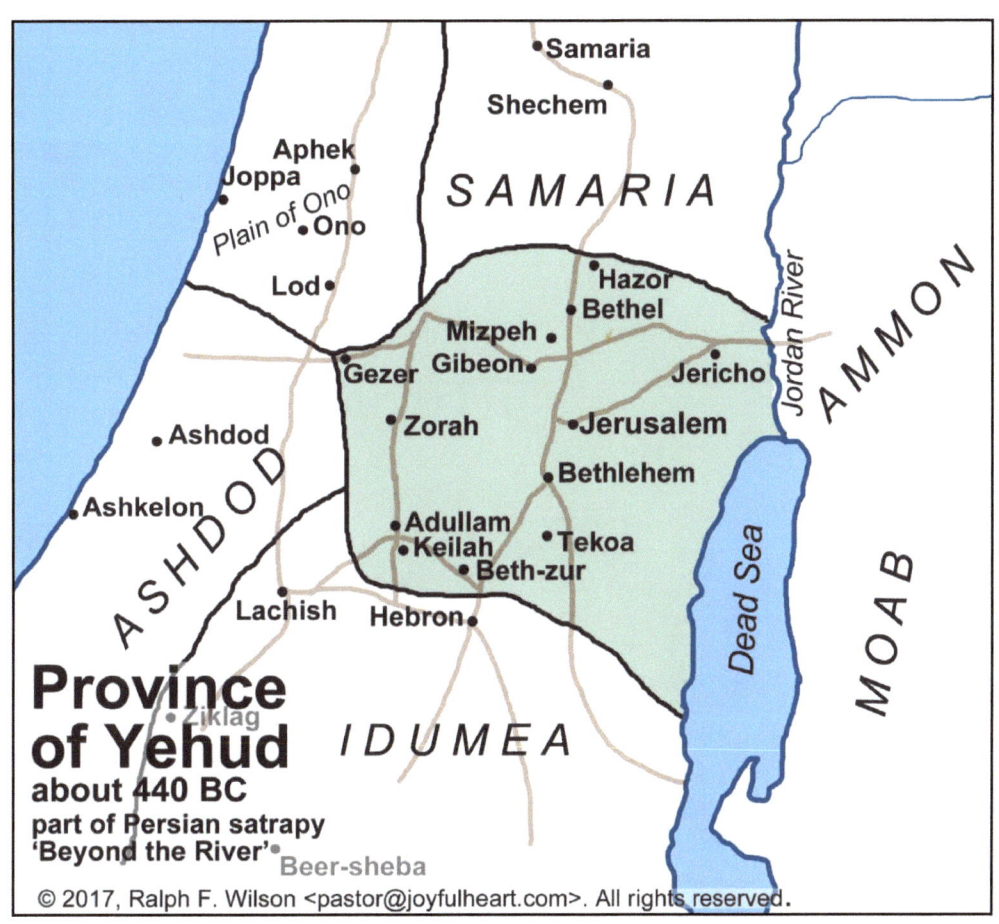

Fig. 8
Map of the Persian Province of Yehud, c. 440 BCE. Courtesy of Dr. Ralph Wilson.

Judaea was part of the Persian empire from the 6th - 4th centuries BCE. During the latter part of this period, small silver coins were struck by an autonomous Jewish authority with the permission of the Persians. Many copied the owl design of the popular Athenian silver coins, but the Greek inscription "AθE" was replaced by an ancient Hebrew legend "YEHUD," the Persian name of the Province of Judaea.

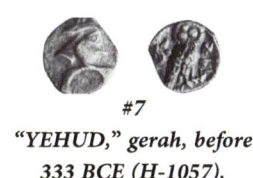

#7
"YEHUD," gerah, before 333 BCE (H-1057).

Fig. 9
Athens, tetradrachm, 454-404 BCE.

Mel Wacks 15

#8
"Yehezqiyah the Governor," half-ma'ah-obol, c. 333-302 BCE (H-1069).

#9
Quarter shekel, before 333 BCE (H-1045). © The Trustees of the British Museum.

Some of these early coins are inscribed in paleo-Aramaic "Yehezqiyah the Governor" (the last governor of Persian Judaea), etc. Josephus mentions a High Priest named Hezekiah who is called "a man of great dignity among his own people" (*Against Appion, 1. 186-199*).

A unique type possibly depicts the Jewish God "Yahweh" in a winged throne. The author hypothesized in a paper *Ezekial's Vision*, prepared for the International Numismatic Congress, New York, 1973: "[This coin portrays] the vision of the prophet Ezekial: 'And upon the likeness of the throne was the likeness … of the glory of the Lord' (*Ezekial 1:26-28*). The deity is shown sitting on a winged wheel just as Ezekial "beheld … one wheel upon the earth by the living creatures)" (*Ezekial 1:15*).

Furthermore, "The head [in the lower right portion of the coin] is the head of the prophet (Ezekial) as described in *Ezekial 1:28*: 'This was the appearance of the likeness of the Lord. And when I saw it, I fell upon my face.'"

Fig. 10
The position of Ezekial's face is very similar to the figure of the Israelite king Jehu bowing down to Shalmaneser III (reigned 858-824 BCE), as shown in this detail from the Black Obelisk from Lachish (c. 700 BCE). © The Trustees of the British Museum.

Donald T. Ariel writes in *A Survey of Coin Finds in Jerusalem (Liber Annuus 32, 1982)*: "Four separate authenticated finds support the theory that the Yehud mint was located in Jerusalem … The Yehud coinage consisted (with one exception) of minute silver coins … It is likely that only such minute coins were needed, serving some now unknown function in the economics of the minting authority. The decision to mint only small coins may also have been influenced by the likelihood that not enough silver bullion existed in the minting authority's treasury to allow for a coinage of large denominations."

The Syrian-Judaean Connection

Fig. 11
Map of Seleucid Palestine, 167 BCE. Courtesy of The Map Archive.

According to the *First Book of Maccabees*, Antiochus VII Sidetes, the Seleucid King of Syria, granted the last of the Maccabee brothers, Simon (142-135 BCE): **"leave also to coin money for thy country with thine own stamp"** (*I Maccabees 15:2-9*). Unfortunately, no Jewish coins of this period are known; perhaps because this right was withdrawn along with other political privileges extended to Simon after his murder and the accession to the throne of his son John

Mel Wacks 17

Hyrcanus I. Antiochus thereupon besieged Jerusalem and extracted a tribute of 500 talents of gold, equivalent to 1 ½ million shekels!

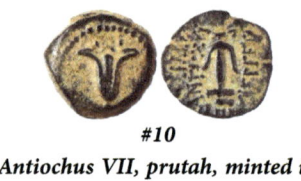

#10
Antiochus VII, prutah, minted in Jerusalem, 131/130 BCE (H-1131).

Coinage was considered an important symbol of sovereignty, and so when Antiochus VII gained sufficient control in Jerusalem, he struck small bronze coins there that appear to be half Jewish, half Seleucid. One side features the Seleucid national emblem — an anchor — with the Greek inscription "Of King Antiochus, Benefactor," and below is the date AπP (Year 181 of the Seleucid era = 132/1 BCE) or the following year BπP. The reverse is a Judaean motif — a lily — a symbol associated with Jerusalem: "And the capitals that (were) upon the top of the pillars (were) of lily work in the porch, four cubits" (*I Kings 7:19*).

Fig. 12
Seleucid Kingdom, Demetrios II Nikator, drachm, 146-138 BCE.

We don't know what these small bronze coins or the similarly sized coins issued by the Hasmoneans were called, but they are now called prutot (prutah, singular). John Lightfoot wrote in 1859 (*Commentary on the New Testament from the Telmud and Hebraica*): "A prutah was the very least piece among coins. Maimonides [wrote] 'That which is not worth a prutah, is not to be reckoned among riches.'"

Maccabees/Hasmoneans

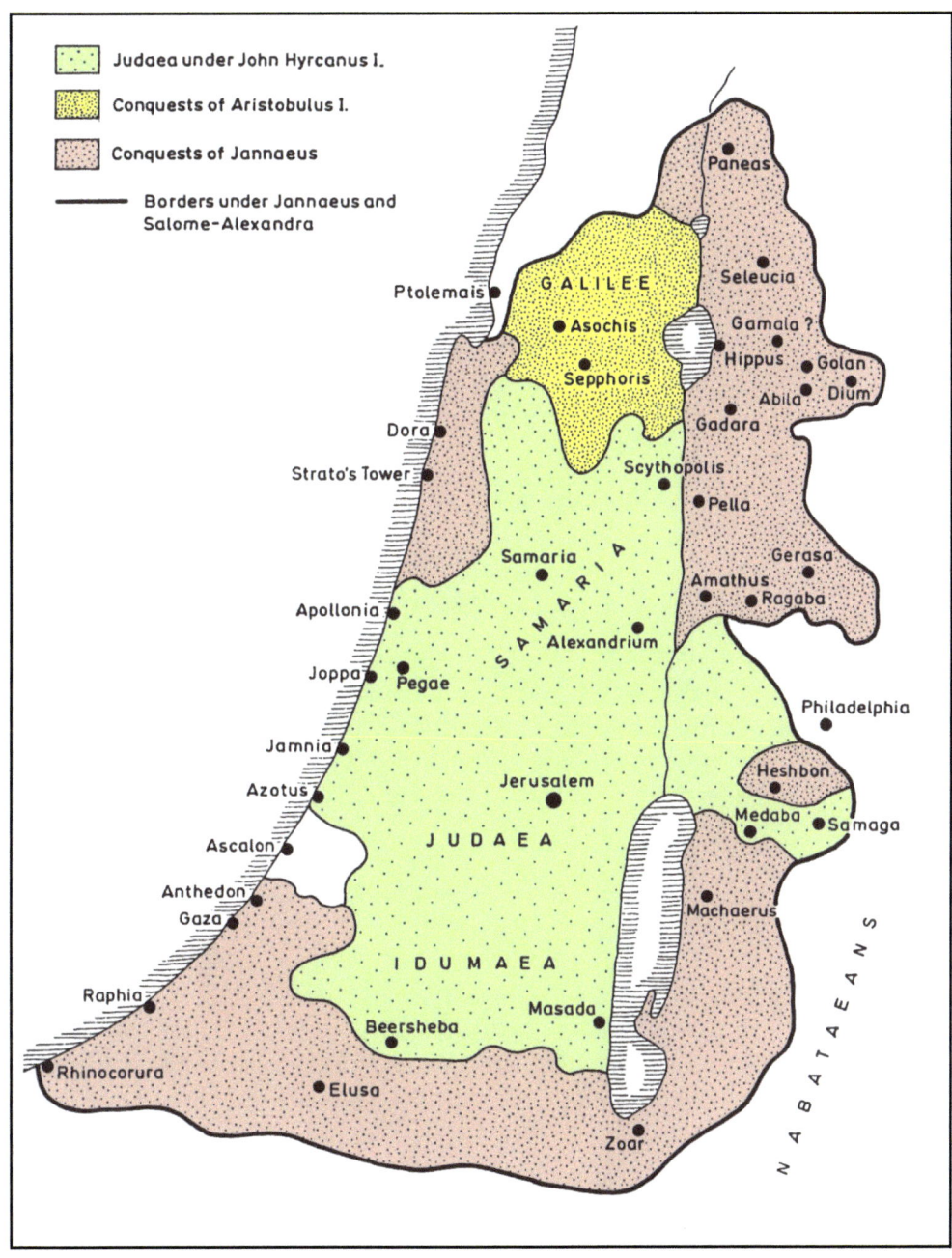

Fig. 13
Map of the Hasmonean Dynasty, 134-76 BCE. Created by Lübke & Wiedemann KG, Leonberg. Courtesy of Fritz Rudolf Künker GmbH & Co. KG, Osnabrück.

Now, at last, we come to the first truly Jewish coins — and a major debate over who issued what and when. I will abide by David Hendin's chronology as published in "Guide to Biblical Coins."

Mel Wacks 19

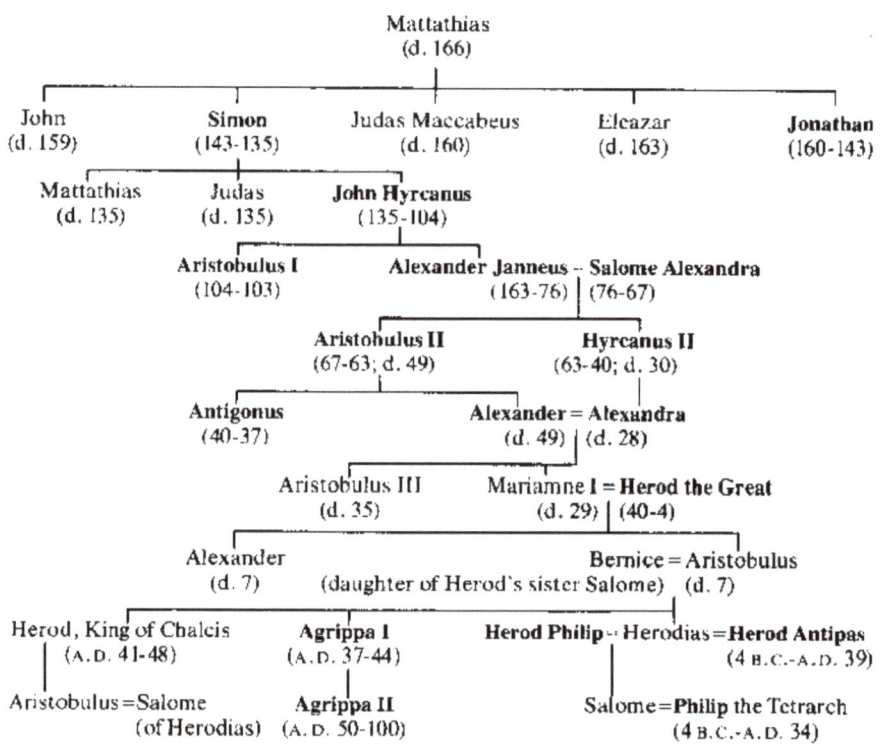

Fig. 14
Maccabean-Hasmonean-Herodian Family Tree.

After the death of Antiochus VII in 129 BCE, John Hyrcanus achieved the complete independence of Judaea, and greatly expanded his kingdom through conquests of Idumaea, Samaria, and parts of Transjordan & the Galilee. The final words in the *Book of Maccabees I* are: "As concerning the rest of the acts of John, and his wars, and worthy deeds which he did, and the building of the walls which he made, and his doings, Behold, these are written in the chronicles of his priesthood, from the time he was made high priest after his father."

#11
John Hyrcanus, 2 prutot,
135-104 BCE (H-1136).

Josephus (*Antiquities* of the Jews, 12:26.3) was the first to call the Maccabees "Hasmoneans," derived from a family ancestor. The first coin issued by the Hasmoneans is thought to have been John Hyrcanus' very rare double prutah, featuring a pair of cornucopia (horns-of-plenty) and a crested helmet — imitating Seleucid coin motifs. The Hebrew inscription reads "Yehochanan the High Priest and Leader of the Community of the Jews."

Fig. 15
Seleucid Kingdom, (L) Alexander II Zabinas, 125–122 BCE, (R) Antiochus VII, 138-129 BCE.

All of the Hasmoneans issued small bronze prutot with double cornucopia on one side and a Hebrew inscription on the other, within a wreath, as follows: "(The name of the Jewish leader) High Priest (Cohen Gadol) and the Council or Community (Chever) of the Jews (Yehudim)." In *Head Decoration Representations on Hasmonean and Herodian Coins* (Israel Numismatic Research, 2013), Ido Noy writes: "As a result of its appearance on Hyrcanus' coins and later on his successors' coins … the wreath gradually acquired the … meanings of leadership and authority."

The reverse design features a poppy — sometimes called a pomegranate — between double cornucopia (see Appendix H ("*Poppies or Pomegranates?*"). In *Ancient Jewish Coinage*, Ya'akov Meshorer explains that "It is logical to assume that the [cornucopia] symbol filtered into Judaism as an object related to fertility, and then acquired additional Jewish connotations … In Jewish life animal horns were used for a number of purposes, including as an oil container, an object to anoint kings, or as 'shofars' — musical instruments of the temple service."

An interesting prutah has a Greek "A" above the Hebrew inscription, possibly referring to an alliance made between John Hyrcanus and Alexander Zabinas (pretender to the Syrian throne) in 128 BCE.

#12
Yehochanan = John Hyrcanus, with "A" above = Alexander Zabinas?, prutah, 135-104 BCE (H-1132).

#13
Yehochanan = John Hyrcanus, prutah, 135-104 BCE (H-1135).

Hyrcanus' successor, Judah Aristobulus, completed the conquest of the Galilee. Under Aristobulus' brother, Alexander Jannaeus, the Jewish kingdom reached its zenith, stretching from Panias to Beer-Sheba, from the Mediterranean coast to the east bank of the Jordan (Transjordan).

#14
Yehudah = Judah Aristobulus, prutah, 104-103 BCE (H-1143).

#15
Yehonatan = Alexander Jannaeus, prutah, 103-76 BCE (H-1146).

#16
"High Priest Yonatan" possibly = Jonathan Hyrcanus II, when his mother Salome Alexandra (76-67 BCE) or he (67, 63-40 BCE) ruled Judaea, prutah, (H-1159).

#17
Alexander Jannaeus, prutah, 103-76 BCE (H-1150 var).

Jannaeus' widow, Salome Alexandra, reigned from 76-67 BCE, but no coins have been attributed to her or her son Hyrcanus II (ruled 67-66 BCE). Perhaps, as proposed by Shlomo Guil (www.academia.edu, 2020): "Salome Alexandra may have refrained from minting coins during the period of her rule due to restrictions which were imposed upon her by the Pharisees [of] objects containing various images which may be attributed to paganism … namely, the coin bearing on the obverse an anchor and on the reverse a star with eight rays … interpreted by them as an outright heavenly body … and the Pharisees therefore decreed that all of these coins, on which they could lay their hands on, be dumped into the Dead Sea" (see Eshel, Zisso 2003 page 92).

The Hasmonean prutah and half prutah bronze coins featuring the anchor/sun-wheel had been made in two major varieties. One has an anchor surrounded by a Greek inscription "King Alexander" combined with a sun-wheel containing an ancient Hebrew inscription "Yehonatan Hamelech" (Alexander Jannaeus the King) between the spokes. The anchor design is imitative of Seleucid coins, while the "sun-wheel" resembles the "Symbol of Vergina," a decorative motif found on Hellenistic coins (including those of Alexander the Great), shields, vases, etc. The motif usually had 16, 12 or 8 "rays" and sometimes it was a religious symbol connected with the 12 Olympian gods.

Fig. 16
(L) Macedonia, c. 300 BCE; (R) Luceria, quincunxlate, 3rd century BCE.

#18
Alexander Jannaeus, with modern square Hebrew inscription around sun-wheel, prutah, 78 BCE (H-1152).

An interesting prutah-type was issued by Jannaeus, that has the same Greek legend surrounding a small anchor, but the reverse has a crude modern square Hebrew inscription around the sun-wheel, reading "King Alexander Year 25." The date refers to the 25th year of Alexander's reign, corresponding to 78 BCE. This is the only ancient Judaean coin with a modern square Hebrew inscription, and also the first dated Jewish coin.

#19
Alexander Jannaeus, half prutah, 103-76 BCE (H-1153).

Half prutah coins were also minted, that are stamped on very irregular planchets — often more rectangular than round — and generally have fragmentary inscriptions, if any.

#20
Alexander Jannaeus, prutah, 103-76 BCE (H-1148).

Another, somewhat scarcer, prutah issued by Jannaeus closely resembles the coins issued in Jerusalem earlier by the Syrian King Antiochus VII — featuring a lily and an anchor.

The Last of the Maccabees

Mattathias Antigonus (40-37 BCE) was the last of the Maccabean-Hasmonean line to rule Judaea. His short but volatile reign was subjected to persistent conflict against Herod the Great. Herod was ultimately victorious, and executed Mattathias at Antioch in 37 BCE. The crudeness of Mattathias' coins are evidence of the desperation of his cause. His small bronze prutot feature double cornucopia, like his predecessors, but his Hebrew name (no title is indicated) is always backwards!

The small bronze prutah of Mattathias has a barley grain between two cornucopia. A medium sized coin depicts a single cornucopia. The large bronze of Mattathias, featuring double cornucopia, is one of the biggest coins issued by the Hasmoneans. Its dual Hebrew and Greek inscriptions tied together the names Antigonus and Mattathias for the first time for historians. These coins had their planchets cast in two halves in a mold, and were generally not precisely aligned when they were struck, giving them a distinctive appearance.

#21
Mattathias Antigonus, prutah, 40-37 BCE (H-1164).

#22
Mattathias Antigonus, 4 prutot, 40-37 BCE (H-1163).

#23
Mattathias Antigonus, 8 prutot, 40-37 BCE (H-1162).

The most famous, and one of the rarest, of all Judaean coins was issued in the final days of Mattathias Antigonus' reign, in a last ditch attempt to rally the Jews against Herod's overwhelming forces. The small coins feature holy ceremonial objects from the Temple of Jerusalem — the seven-branched menorah and table of showbread — symbols that never appeared before or since until the establishment of the State of Israel in 1948.

#24
Mattathias Antigonus, prutah, 40-37 BCE (H-1168).

"And you shall make a menorah of pure gold. The menorah shall be made of hammered work; its base and its stem, its goblets, its knobs, and its flowers shall [all] be [one piece] with it. And six branches coming out of its sides: three menorah branches from its one side and three menorah branches from its second side" (*Exodus 25:31-32*). And you shall make a table of acacia wood, two cubits its length, one cubit its width, and a cubit and a half its height ... And you shall place on the table showbread before Me at all times" (*Exodus 25:23, 30*).

Fig. 17
Both the Temple menorah and the table of showbread (upper right) can be seen on the Arch of Titus (82 CE) in Rome. Source: Arch of Titus Project, Yeshiva University.

The Widow's Mite

Fig. 18
The Widow's Mite. Engraving by Gustave Doré.

The story of the "Widow's Mite" tells how, in 30 CE, "Jesus sat over against the (temple) treasury, and beheld how the people cast money into the treasury; and many that were rich cast in much. And there came a certain poor widow, and she threw in two mites ... And he called unto him his disciples, and saith unto them ... that this poor widow hath cast more in than all they which have cast into the treasury. For all they did cast in of their abundance; but she did cast in all that she had, even all her living" (*Mark 12:41-44*).

The most likely candidates for the "two mites" are the only small bronze Jewish coins that were available — the common prutot and half prutot (#12-20) issued by the Hasmoneans (135 - 37 BCE).

Even though these were issued about 70-160 years before this event, it should be noted that these coins often circulated for hundreds of years in ancient times, as evidenced by the generally low grades of those that have survived.

So, where did the word "mite" come from? It does not have an ancient origin. When the English clerics and scholars who translated the King James Version of the Bible (published in 1611) came to this parable, they faced a problem. There was no English word for such a tiny denomination. Old arithmetic books, however, referred to a unit of account worth half a farthing, the "mite."

This was based on an actual coin, the mijt, weighing less than a gram, which circulated across the Channel in Flanders in the 14th and 15th centuries. Originally struck in billon, a low-grade silver-copper alloy, it gradually declined to a tiny copper piece. These are relatively rare, since they had a low survival rate.

Fig. 19
Brabant, Philips de Goede, mijte, c. 1466-1467.

A Tale of Three Camels

Fig. 20
Map of the Nabataean Kingdom, c. 85 BCE. Courtesy of F. Villeneuve & L. Nehmé.

The Romans had a long history of interfering with Judaean affairs, as they did with other peoples throughout their sphere of influence. These actions often were reflected on Roman coins. Three such issues were Roman silver denarii that deal with historic events involving Hasmonean kings.

#25
Roman Republic, Marcus Aemilius Scaurus, "Rex Aretas," denarius, 58 BCE (H-1441).

The first "camel coin," issued in 58 BCE, carries the inscriptions "M SCAVR AED CVR / EX S C / REX ARETAS" on the obverse and "P HVPSAEVS AED CVR / [CAPTV] / C HVPSAE COS PREIVER" on the reverse. M SCAVR = Marcus Aemilius Scaurus; AED CVR = Scaurus' title, Aedile Curulis, indicating that he was responsible for organizing public celebrations in Rome; EX SC = issued by consent of the Roman Senate; HVPSAEVS = the consul Gaius Hypsaeus, who was an ancestor of Scaurus; CAPTV / C HVPSAE COS PREIVER = captured the Volscian town of Privernum.

It was a tradition to commemorate the deeds of an ancestor on coins of the period, however Scaurus also depicted an event from his own career, the first such instance in Roman coinage. The kneeling figure represents the Nabataean King Aretas III. Aretas had allied himself with John Hyrcanus II, while the Romans favored Hyrcanus' brother Aristobulus II. About 50 BCE, the Greek historian Diodorus Siculus wrote: "Just as the Seleucids had tried to subdue [the Nabataeans], so the Romans made several attempts to get their hands on that lucrative trade."

While serving as Governor of Syria, Scaurus invaded Nabataea, laying waste much of its territory. Although he was unable to conquer King Aretas' stronghold, through an intermediary he was able to convince Aretas to pay a substantial bribe (300 talents) for him to desist. As the 65 BCE event is presented on the coin one would think that the Nabataeans were soundly defeated and that Aretas begged for mercy, but this is mere propagandistic opportunism on the part of Scaurus.

Fig. 21
Nabataea, Aretas III, Damascus Mint, 85 BCE.

#26
Roman Republic, Marcus Aemilius Scaurus, denarius, 58 BCE (H-1442).

The second "camel coin," also issued in 58 BCE by Marcus Aemilius Scaurus, has nearly identical designs — but the name of "Rex Aretas" has been removed from the obverse, while the reverse inscriptions are virtually unchanged. Could this have been done because the Romans realized that the victory over Aretas was *Fake News*?

In 54 BCE, a denarius that was similar in concept to the Rex Aretas coin was issued by the Roman curule aedile Aulus Plautius. The reverse design features a kneeling figure offering an olive branch and holding a camel by the bridle; the inscription is "BACCHIVS IVDAEVS" (Bacchius the Jew), whose actual identity is still unknown.

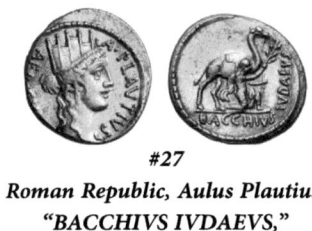

#27
Roman Republic, Aulus Plautius, "BACCHIVS IVDAEVS," denarius, 54 BCE (H-1443).

Much has been written about the possible identification of Bacchius Judaeus, such as this early article in the July, 1903 Spink & Son's Monthly Numismatic Circular:

"The most probable explanation of this somewhat enigmatic legend is that the Romans thought Bacchus was worshipped by the Jews. Just as the priest of Hercules was called Herculius, so the priest of Bacchus would be called Bacchius. Now it was well known that Aristobulus was both King and High Priest of the Jews, hence under the figure representing Aristobulus we find the name Bacchius Judaeus. Plutarch wrote a chapter to identify Bacchus with the God of the Jews.

Among the reasons which the Romans had for this curious idea that the Jews worshipped Bacchus was that Epiphanius supposedly found in the temple an ass's head which was a symbol of Bacchus (*Tac. Hist. V, 4*). Niconor [general under Demetrius I, in conducting the war against Judas Maccabaeus], threatened the priests that "**he would raze the temple of God even with the ground, break down the altar, and erect there a temple unto Bacchus (Dionysus) for all to see**" (*2 Maccabees 14:33*).

Joseph, son of Tobias, tried to institute in Jerusalem a feast of Bacchus. [*2 Maccabees 7* indicates: "**when the feast of Bacchus was kept, they were compelled to go about crowned with ivy in honor of Bacchus.**"]

Fig. 22
Feast of Bacchus in Jerusalem, engraving published 1886.

Aristobulus sent Pompey as a gift the golden vine of the temple, worth 500 talents; Josephus tells us it was placed in the Temple of Jupiter Capitolinus. The opinion of the Romans is plainly expressed by Tacitus (*Hist. V, 5*): "A vine wrought in gold was seen in their temple hence some have inferred that Bacchus the conqueror of the East was the object of their adoration. But the Jewish forms of worship have no conformity with the rites of Bacchus."

These considerations lead us to look upon the supplicant kneeling by the camel, on the coin of Plautius, as a portrait of Aristobulus. Other guesses of numismatists were that some Arab king was meant whose name was Bacchius, or that Bacchius was the Latinized form of the name Dionysios, the tyrant of Tripolis. The Duc de Luynes thought that Bacchius was a Latin form of the Hebrew name of Aristobulus. The true identification of Bacchius Judaeus remains an intriguing mystery.

"Judaea Capta" Precursor

What are the odds that a single example of an ancient coin type will survive over 2000 years? It does happen, such as the unique 36 BCE denarius issued by Gaius Sosius, General under Mark Antony (yes, that Mark Antony, the friend of Julius Caesar), who is depicted on the obverse. The reverse is inscribed "C•SOSIVS IMP, "and pictures two Jewish captives — a woman on the right and a male (possibly representing Mattathias Antigonus) on the left — seated beneath a Roman trophy — with a shield hanging on the right and a spear on the left. It was originally pictured in 1908 in *Journal International d'Archéologie Numismatique*, Tome onzième, pl. XIII, p. 231, Svoronos.

#28
Roman Republic, with Mark Antony, issued by Gaius Sosius, denarius, 36 BCE (H-1444).

This remarkable coin celebrated Roman victory over Judaean forces about 100 years before the extensive series of Judaea Capta coins issued later by Rome. This time, it commemorated the triumph of Roman forces backing Herod the Great against the last of the Hasmonean kings, Mattathias Antigonus.

We will never know what the main antagonists — Mattathias Antigonus and Herod the Great — looked like, because of the Jewish prohibition of graven images, however the portraits of Mark Antony and Gaius Sosius are available on this and other coins.

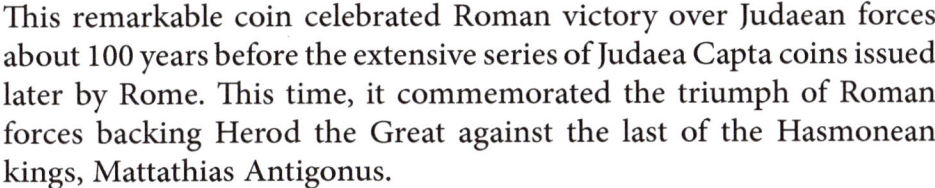

Fig. 23
(L) Mark Antony, aureus, 41 BCE, (R) Gaius Sosius, struck at unknown Asia Minor mint, 39 BCE.

Here is how Josephus described these events in *Of the War — Book I, Chapter 1:*

"Indeed though they had so great an army lying round about them, they bore a siege of five months, till some of Herod's chosen men ventured to get upon the wall, and fell into the city, as did Sosius's centurions after them; and now they first of all seized upon what was about the temple, and upon the pouring in of the army, there was slaughter of vast multitudes everywhere … Then it was that

Mel Wacks 31

Antigonus, without any regard to his former or to his present fortune, came down from the citadel, and fell down at Sosius's feet, who, without pitying him at all, upon the change of his condition, laughed at him beyond measure ... Yet did he ... put him into bonds, and kept him in custody ... Hereupon Sosius dedicated a crown of gold to God, and then went away from Jerusalem, leading Antigonus away in bonds to Antony: then did the axe bring him to his end, who still had a fond desire of life, and some frigid hopes of it to the last, but by his cowardly behaviour well deserved to die by it."

Herod the Great

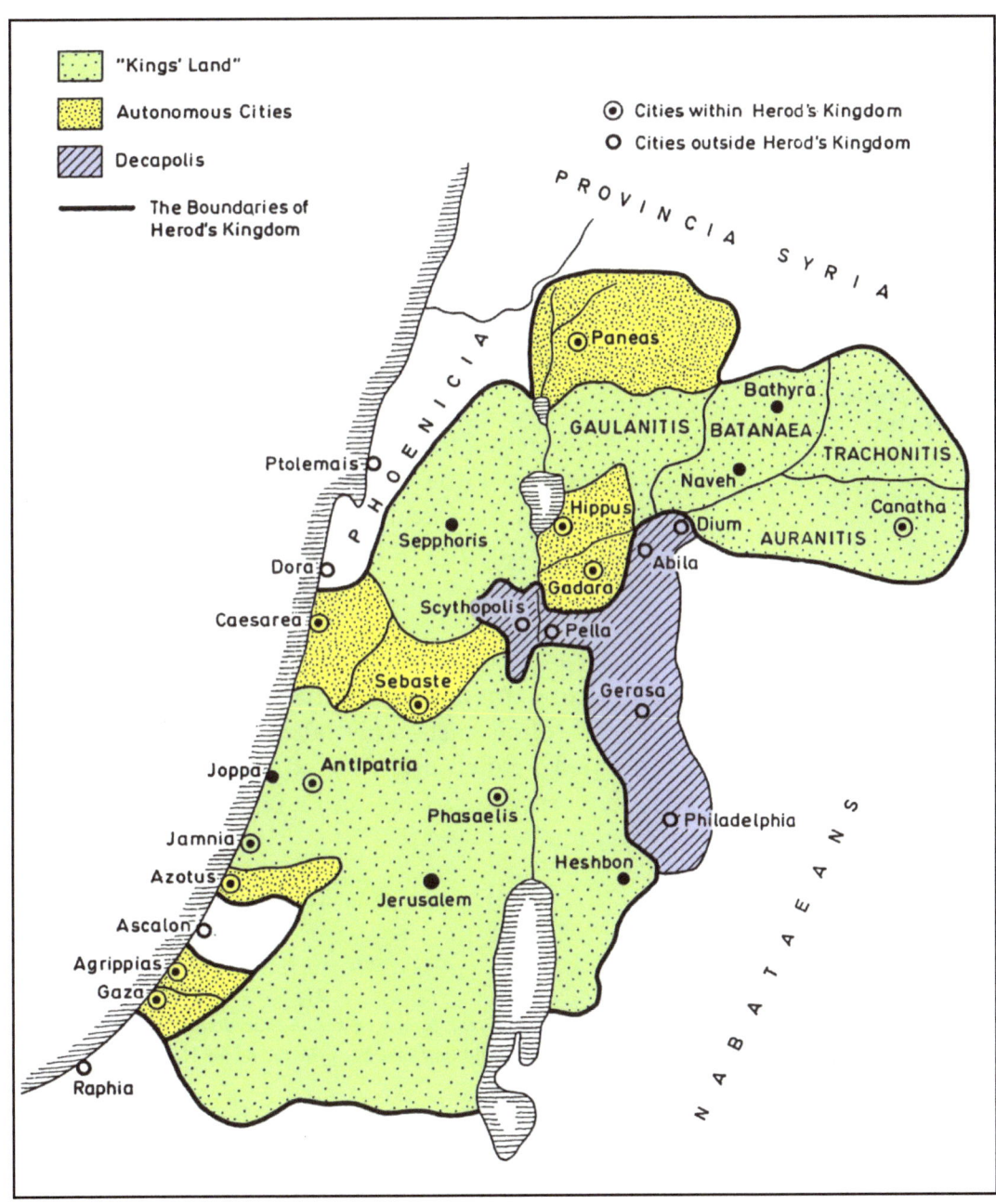

Fig. 24
Map of Herod the Great, 37-4 BCE, Created by Lübke & Wiedemann KG, Leonberg.
Courtesy of Fritz Rudolf Künker GmbH & Co. KG, Osnabrück.

During the rule of John Hyrcanus II (47-40 BCE), Antipater — an Idumaean whose family had converted to Judaism when Hyrcanus' father ruled — was appointed by Julius Caesar as the first governor of Judaea. Idumaeans lived in Edom — a country bordering Judaea — in what is now southwest Jordan, between the Dead Sea and the Gulf of Aqaba. The Idumeans were descendents of Esau (oldest son of Isaac) according to *Genesis 36:9*: "This is the genealogy of Esau the father of the Edomites." Antipater chose his younger son, Herod, who was still only a boy, as governor of Galilee. When the last Hasmonean king, Mattathias Antigonus, was defeated and executed by order of Mark Antony, Herod became the undisputed ruler of Judaea. When he was told that another "King of the Jews" was born: "Herod ... was exceedingly wroth, and sent forth and slew all the children that were in Bethlehem, and in all the coasts thereof, from two years and under" (*Matthew 2:16*).

#29
Herod the Great, prutah, 37-4 BCE (H-1188).

The most common coin of Herod the Great is similar to Hasmonean coins — an anchor with Greek inscription "HPω BACI" (King Herod), and a double cornucopia — but with a caduceus (associated with a pagan god) in between, instead of a pomegranate.

#30
Herod the Great, prutah, 37-4 BCE (H-1190).

Herod's coins feature innovative designs which, while not truly Jewish in character, at least do not feature any human likeness. However, it is on one of Herod the Great's small bronze coins that a living thing is depicted for the first time since the Persian period. The eagle probably commemorates this event: "Now the king had put up a golden eagle over the great gate of the temple" (*Josephus, War of the Jews I:33*).

#31
Herod the Great, 2 prutot, 37-4 BCE (H-1171).

Objects pictured on other Herodian coins include a winged caduceus and a poppy (often mistakenly called a pomegranate — see Appendix H), a plumed helmet and a shield, and a cross within a diadem (a headband worn as a crown), and a tripod table.

#32
Herod the Great, 4 prutot, 37-4 BCE (H-1170).

Fig. 25
Alexander the Great, bronze coin with Macedonian helmet and shield, 336-323 BCE. Could this have been the model for Herod the Great's coins?

#33
Herod the Great, 2 prutot, 37-4 BCE (H-1178).

The largest coin of Herod features unusual designs — a helmet with long cheek pieces, topped by a star, on the obverse; and a tripod holding a ceremonial bowl, on the reverse. This coin, along with the coin depicting a smaller helmet, both feature dates (LΓ = Year 3), indicating the third year of Herod's reign (37 BCE). In 40 BCE, Herod was granted the governorship of Judaea by the Roman Senate, however it was not until 3 years later that Herod became king in fact as well as in name.

#34
Herod the Great, 8 prutot,
37-4 BCE (H-1169).

The Herodian Dynasty

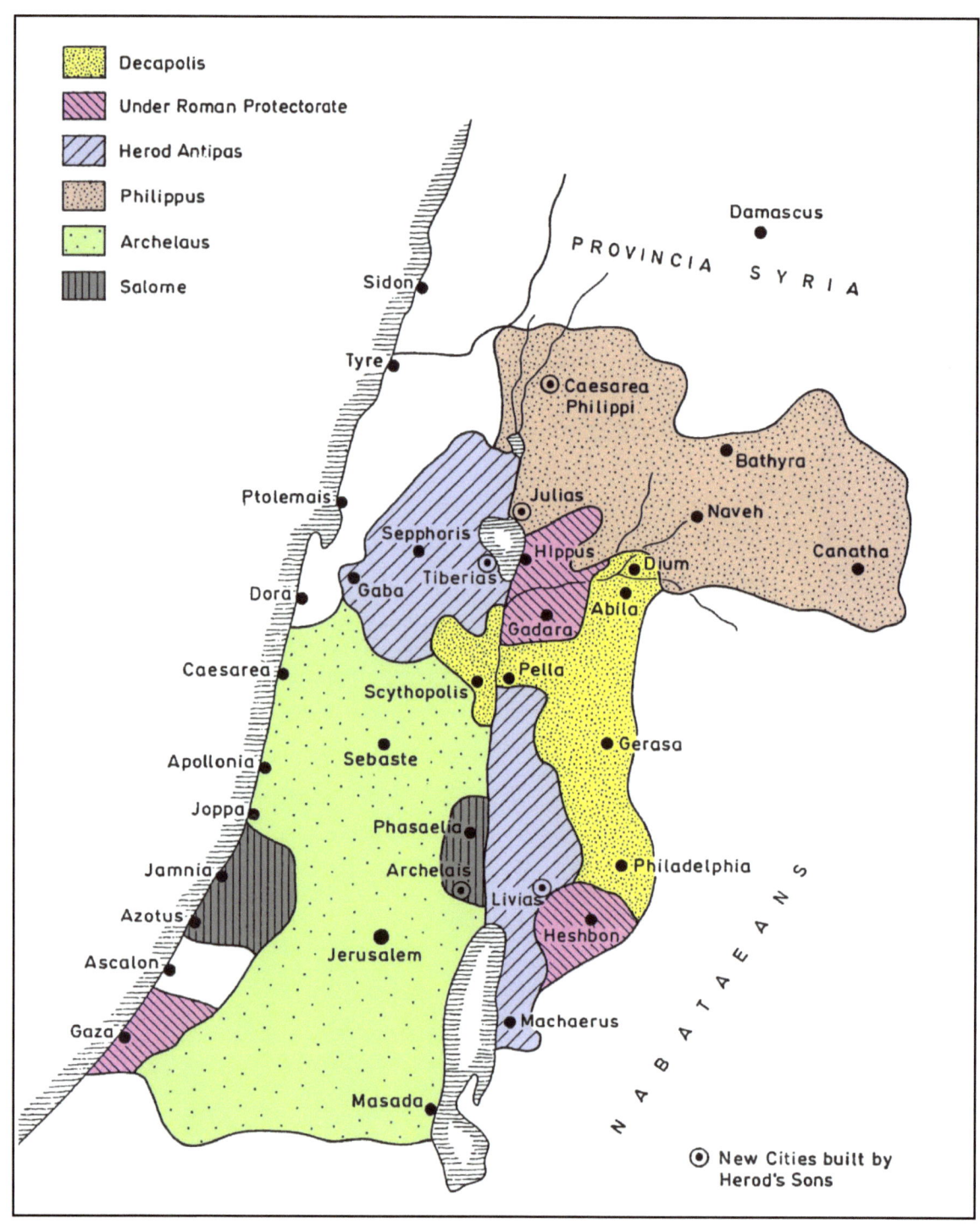

Fig. 26
Map of the Herodian Dynasty & Roman Prefects/Procurators, 4 BCE-39 CE. Created by Lübke & Wiedemann KG, Leonberg. Courtesy of Fritz Rudolf Künker GmbH & Co. KG, Osnabrück.

After Herod's death in 4 BCE, the Roman Emperor Augustus divided the Jewish kingdom among Herod's three sons. Archelaus was appointed ethnarch ("Ruler of the Nation") over Judaea, Idumaea (the original homeland of his family), and Samaria. "When Herod (the Great) was dead, behold an angel of the Lord appeareth in a dream of Joseph in Egypt ... But when he heard that Archelaus did reign in Judaea in the room of his father Herod, he was afraid to go thither" (*Matthew 2:19-23*).

Herod Antipas received purely Jewish but widely separated areas — Galilee and Peraea (Jewish Transjordan). And the third son, Herod Philip, was given predominantly non-Jewish settlements in Syria. This was reflected in their coinage — no living things appear on the coins of Archelaus and Antipas, but Philip became the first Jewish ruler to place a portrait (of his benefactor, the Roman Emperor Augustus) on his coins.

The most common coins of Herod Archelaus (4 BCE - 6 CE) are the small prutot featuring a bunch of grapes and a crested helmet with his name and title spelled out in Greek, and coins with a ship's prow and wreath with his name and title abbreviated.

#35
Herod Archelaus, prutah, 4 BCE-6 CE (H-1196).

#36
Herod Archelaus, prutah, 4 BCE-6 CE (H-1197).

A scarce double prutah of Herod Archelaus pictures a galley ship and conjoined double cornucopia, inscribed in Greek with his name and title.

#37
Herod Archelaus, double prutah, 4 BCE-6 CE (H-1194).

Antipas plays a key role in the New Testament, adding to the desirability of his coins: "And King Herod (Antipas) heard of him (for his name was spread abroad) and he said, that John the Baptist was risen from the dead" (*Mark 6:14*). The rare coins of Herod Antipas (4 BCE - 39 CE) generally feature an upright palm branch surrounded by the Greek inscription "Herod the Tetrarch." The name of the city — Tiberias (named by Antipas after the Roman Emperor Tiberius) — where the coins were minted, is contained within a wreath on the reverse.

#38
Herod Antipas, mint of Tiberias, full denomination, 20/21 CE (H-1199).

Mel Wacks 37

#39
Herod Philip II, with Emperor Tiberius, 30/31 CE (H-1230).

#40
Herod Philip II, Caesarea Philippi, 30/31 CE (H-1232).

The coins of Herod Philip II (4 BCE - 34 CE) generally depict a portrait of the Roman Emperor on the obverse and the facade of a tetrastyle (four columns) temple on the reverse; they are all dated according to the Emperor's regnal year.

A rare coin depicting the portrait of Herod Philip himself, when he was about 55 years old, was struck in 30/31 CE in Caesarea Philippi. This is the first coin to feature a portrait of a Jewish ruler.

Philip II, sometimes called Philip the Tetrarch, was married to the infamous Salome — but more about her later.

Herod's Grandchildren

Fig. 27
Map of the Territory of Agrippa II, the Roman Prefects/Procurators, and Chalcis, 6-96 CE.

In 37 CE, Rome gave the lands of Herod Philip II to Herod Agrippa I, the grandson of Herod the Great and Miriam (of the Hasmonean line). When Herod Antipas was banished two years later, his territory also was assigned to Agrippa. By 41 CE, Agrippa I — descendent of both the Maccabees and Herod the Great — became the sole ruler of Judaea. Apparently, it is Agrippa I who is referred to in the Mishnah (Jewish Oral Law): When celebrating the Festival of the First Fruits "even King Agrippa carried the baskets (of fruit) on his shoulder" (*Bikkurim 3:4*). It was also Herod Agrippa I who "stretched forth his hands to vex certain of the church. And he killed James the brother of John with the sword. And ... he proceeded further to take Peter also" (*Acts 12:1-3*).

#41
Herod Agrippa I, prutah,
42/43 CE (H-1244).

The most common coin of Agrippa was also the only coin issued for circulation in his Jewish territories. This bronze prutah shows a royal umbrella on the obverse surrounded by the Greek inscription "King Agrippa;" the reverse features three ears of barley and the date "LS", Year 6 = 42/43 CE.

All of the other coins of Herod Agrippa I contain graven images — portraits of the Emperor or even the Jewish ruler himself. One rarity features a portrait of Agrippa along with his son Agrippa II on horseback.

#42
Herod Agrippa I, Year 2 =
37/38 CE (H-1237).

Other grandchildren and relatives of Herod the Great ruled over pagan areas by the will of Imperial Rome. One descendent, Tigranes, was a king of Armenia (more about him in the next chapter), and another Herod received the throne of Chalcis (ancient Syria). Herod of Chalcis (41-48 CE) was also appointed the High Priest, and was guardian of the Jewish Temple in Jerusalem. Both Herod of Chalcis and his son Aristobulus of Chalcis (57-92 CE) felt no need to heed the Jewish prohibition of portraits on the coins issued for their pagan territories, and so their likenesses appeared. One rarity features a portrait of Aristobulus' infamous wife — Salome — daughter of Herod Philip. "When Herod's birthday was kept, the daughter [Salome] of Herodias danced before them, and pleased Herod [Antipas]" (*Matthew 14:6*). This coin, coincidentally, was issued in an historically significant year — at the start of the First Revolt.

#43
Aristobulus of Chalcis and his wife
Salome, 66/67 CE (H-1257a).

40 The Handbook of Biblical Numismatics

The last ruler of the Herodian line — Agrippa II — reigned for an impressive 45 years (50-c.95 CE). This is the "Agrippa (who) said unto Paul, almost thou persuades me to be a Christian" (*Acts 26:28*). Coins issued by Agrippa II include both Jewish (with palm branch) and pagan (with Roman goddess) types.

#44
Agrippa II, struck in Tiberias, 53 CE (H-1266).

#45
Agrippa II, with portrait of Emperor Vespasian and a Roman goddess, 86 CE (H-1282).

The Herodian Kings of Armenia

Fig. 28
Map of the Armenian Kingdom, c. 66 BCE.

The father of Tigranes V was a son of Herod the Great and his wife Mariamne; his mother was a Cappadocian Princess. Tigranes was born and raised in Herod's court in Jerusalem. After the death of Herod in 4 BCE, Tigranes and his brother left Jerusalem to live with their mother and her family in the Cappadocian Royal Court. Soon after, Tigranes and his brother deserted their Jewish religion.

After the death of Artavasdes IV in 6 CE, Emperor Augustus appointed Tigranes as King of Armenia. Soon after, Tigranes co-ruled with Queen Erato, until 12 CE, when they were overthrown for unknown reasons.

A great-grandson of Herod the Great, Tigranes VI was raised as a royal hostage in Rome and crowned by Nero as king of Armenia around 58 CE. Tigranes invaded a neighboring small vassal state of the Parthians and deposed their king. Parthia considered this as an act of aggression from Rome, and attacked Armenia. Parthia was victorious, and signed a treaty with Rome to install Tiridates I as King of Armenia. In 63 CE, Tigranes renounced his crown. There is evidence that Nero planned to restore Tigranes to the Armenian throne, however this was abandoned with the outbreak of the First Revolt in 66 CE.

#46
Kingdom of Armenia, Tigranes V, dichalkon, 6-12 CE (H-Fig. 7.9).

#47
Kingdom of Armenia, Tigranes VI, chalkous, 60-62 CE (H-Fig. 7.9).

The Prefects & Procurators

Roman-appointed prefects governed in Judaea (6-41 and 44-48 CE), with Herod Agrippa I ruling briefly in the interim. The Roman governor was called "procurator" from 48-66 CE. As a rule, their official residence was in Caesarea, except during Jewish festivals when they stayed in Jerusalem.

The initial indifference, and later open hostility, of the prefects and later the procurators, to their Jewish subjects eventually led to a revolt against Rome in 66 CE. Somewhat surprising, in light of their poor attitude towards the Jews, the small bronze prutot issued by the prefects abided by the strict interpretation of the Commandment against graven images: **"You shall not make for yourself a graven image, nor any manner of likeness of anything that is in heaven above, that is in the earth beneath, or that is in the water under the earth"** (*Exodus 20:4*). Except for the pagan religious symbols on the coins of Pontius Pilate the designs were probably not objectionable to the citizenry.

The first design introduced by the prefect Coponius (6-9 CE) — the palm tree — had heretofore appeared only on rare coins of Herod Antipas. The palm tree ultimately became the quintessential symbol of Judaea on coins issued by the Jews during the First and Second Revolts, as well as later Roman-issued Judaean-related pieces. The next prefect, Ambibulus (9-12 CE) continued the palm tree and ear of barley designs. The Latin inscription is the Emperor's title — KAICAP (Caesar). It should be noted that all prefect and procurator coins can be precisely dated since the regnal year (A=1, B=2, etc.) of the Roman Emperor is indicated following the letter "L".

#48
[First name unknown] Coponius, prutah, 5/6 CE (H-1328).

#49
Marcus Ambibulus, prutah, 8/9 CE (H-1329).

#50
Marcus Ambibulus, prutah, 9/10 CE (H-1330).

#51
Marcus Ambibulus, prutah, 10/11 CE (H-1331).

Annius Rufus (12-15 CE) evidently did not issue any coins. However, Valerius Gratus (15-26 CE), prefect under Emperor Tiberius, issued numerous prutot during his long rule. Gratus' coins feature double cornucopia (reverted back to the familiar Hasmonean and Herodian coin motif), upright leafy branch, three lilies, grape vine leaf, amphora, and palm branch. All of these prutot are inscribed with the name of the Emperor Tiberius or his mother Julia (IOYLIA), and the regnal year.

#52
Valerius Gratus, prutah, 15/16 CE (H-1332).

#53
Valerius Gratus, prutah, 15/16 CE (H-1333).

#54
Valerius Gratus, prutah, 16/17 CE (H-1334).

#55
Valerius Gratus, prutah, 16/17 CE (H-1335).

#56
Valerius Gratus, prutah, 17/18 CE (H-1336).

#57
Valerius Gratus, prutah, 17/18 CE (H-1337).

#58
Valerius Gratus, prutah, 17/18 CE (H-1338).

#59
Valerius Gratus, prutah, 18/19 CE (H-1339).

#60
Valerius Gratus, prutah, 24/25 CE (H-1340).

Philo of Alexandria (c. 20 BCE – c. 50 CE) depicted the next prefect — Pontius Pilate — appointed by Tiberius, as "by nature unyielding and of a stubborn harshness." During his rule (26-36 CE) two new coin types appeared that include pagan religious symbols. The first has three ears of barley surrounded by the legend IOYLIA KAICAPOC (Julia Caesar, wife of the Emperor), and a simpulum (Roman ceremonial dipper) with the Emperor's name and regnal year. The second type was introduced in the same year (30/31 CE) that *"… they bound [Jesus] and led him away and delivered him over to Pilate the governor"* (*Matthew 27:2*). These prutot feature a curved litiuus (augur's wand), which was used by certain Roman priests to determine the future. Pilate was the only prefect or procurator to use pagan ceremonial objects on his coins. The simpulum and litiuus also appeared frequently on Roman coins.

Fig. 29
Marcus Brutus, after the assassination of Julius Caesar, features a simpulum in the center of the obverse and an augur's wand is shown on the right of the reverse, denarius, 44 BCE.

Note that Pontius Pilate's title was traditionally thought to have been procurator, since Tacitus speaks of him as such. However, an inscription on a limestone block, known as the "Pilate Stone," that was discovered in 1961 in the ruins of an amphitheater at Caesarea Maritima, refers to Pilate as "Prefect of Judaea."

Fig. 30
The partial inscription on the "Pilate Stone" reads:
[DIS AUGUSTI]S TIBERIÉUM
[…PO]NTIUS PILATUS
[…PRAEF]ECTUS IUDA[EA]E
[…FECIT D]E[DICAVIT]

Pontius Pilate was suspended from his office by Lucius Vitellius, Roman governor of Syria, after Pilate's forces had brutally quashed a gathering of Samaritans on Mount Gerizim. Pilate was succeeded by Marcellus (36-37 CE) and Marullus (37-41 CE), who left no mark in history (including no coins). The next three governors of Judaea, appointed by Emperor Claudius, also did not mint coins: prefects Cuspius Fadus (44-46 CE) and Tiberius Alexander (46-48 CE), and procurator Ventidus Cumanus (48-52 CE). The fires of revolt were lit by the heavy-handed actions of Cumanus, who was eventually deposed and exiled by Claudius.

#61
Pontius Pilate, prutah, 29/30 CE (H-1341).

Nikos Kokkinos writes in *The Prefects of Judaea 6-48 CE and the Misty Period 6-36 CE* (*Judaea and Rome in Coins*, Spinks, 2012): "The change of title from praefectus to procurator for equestrian governors under Claudius, took place, in the case of Judaea, arguably after 48 CE and before or by 52 CE."

#62
Pontius Pilate, prutah, 30/31 CE (H-1342).
(Note: on some coins date is incorrectly inscribed as "LIS").

Procurator Antonius Felix (52-59 CE) married a member of the Jewish royal family — Drusilla — sister of Herod Agrippa II. Unfortunately, reports the historian Tacitus, Felix acted as if he had arrived in a country which existed only to be exploited for his own advantage, and after a tumultuous period he was recalled by Rome. The small bronze coins of Felix introduce new types: crossed palm branches, and crossed shields with a palm tree. The first coin issued by Felix carries the names of the Emperor Claudius and his wife (who was also his niece) Agrippina; the second type features the names of Nero and his brother Britannicus (poisoned by Nero in 55 CE).

#63
Pontius Pilate, prutah, 31/32 CE (H-1343).

#64
Antonius Felix, prutah, 54 CE (H-1347).

Scholarship by Ya'akov Meshorer indicates that "Festus apparently assumed office in 59 CE. His only issue ... was struck immediately upon his arrival in Judaea." These coins feature a palm branch and the Emperor Nero's name. Festus showed sensitivity to his Jewish subjects, but it was he who "said with a loud voice, Paul, thou art beside thyself; much learning doth make thee mad" (*Acts 26:24*).

#65
Antonius Felix, prutah, 54 CE (H-1348).

There was a substantial amount of interplay between the Jewish kings and the procurators: "And after certain days king Agrippa (Herod Agrippa II) and Bernice came unto Caesarea to salute Festus. And when they had been there many days, Festus declared Paul's cause unto the king, saying, There is a certain man left in bonds by Felix" (*Acts 25:13-14*).

#66
Gessius Festus, prutah, 59 CE (H-1351).

No coins are known of the last two procurators — Albinus (62-64 CE) and Gessius Florus (64-66 CE). The brief rule of Albinus completely undid the little good his predecessor had accomplished. The historian Josephus wrote: "There was no sort of wickedness that he did not have a hand in. In his political capacity, he stole and plundered everyone's substance." About Albinus' successor, Tacitus wrote: "Jewish patience lasted until the coming of Gessius Florus." Florus committed acts of flagrant injustice, giving free rein to thieves, and reducing whole communities to misery. Thus a revolt was virtually inevitable.

Mel Wacks 47

The Tribute Penny

Fig. 31
The Tribute Penny. Engraving by Gustave Doré.

In Jesus' time, there was a tax collected (tribute) for the Roman emperor, in addition to the numerous local Judaean taxes. During one of these collections, Jesus said: "Shew me the tribute money. And they brought unto him a penny (King James translation for a silver denarius). And he saith unto them, Whose is this image and superscription? They say unto him, Caesar's. Then saith he unto them, Render therefore unto Caesar the things which are Caesar's, and unto God the things that are God's" (*Matthew 22:19-21*).

The word "penny" was used instead of "denarius" (which was specified as *dēnarion* in the original Greek text), because the English penny was the most commonly used silver coin at the time of the publication of the King James Bible (1611).

Fig. 32
England, King James, penny, 1604-1619.

The coin referred to is generally considered to be a silver Roman denarius featuring the likeness of the Emperor Tiberius (14-37 CE) on one side, and his mother Livia, seated on a throne, on the reverse. However, only a handful of Tiberius' denarii have been found in archaeological digs in the Holy Land — so perhaps the "Tribute Penny" was actually another coin type — such as the Roman denarius of Augustus Caesar with the Caius and Lucius Caesar reverse (2 BCE – 12 CE), as suggested by Rev. Peter Dunstan & Walter Holt (*The Tribute Penny Debate Revisited, The Celator, October, 2006*), and others.

#67
Emperor Tiberius, "The Tribute Penny," denarius, 14-37 CE (H-1622).

Fig. 33
Emperor Augustus, "Alternate Tribute Penny," denarius, 2 BCE–12 CE.

The First Revolt

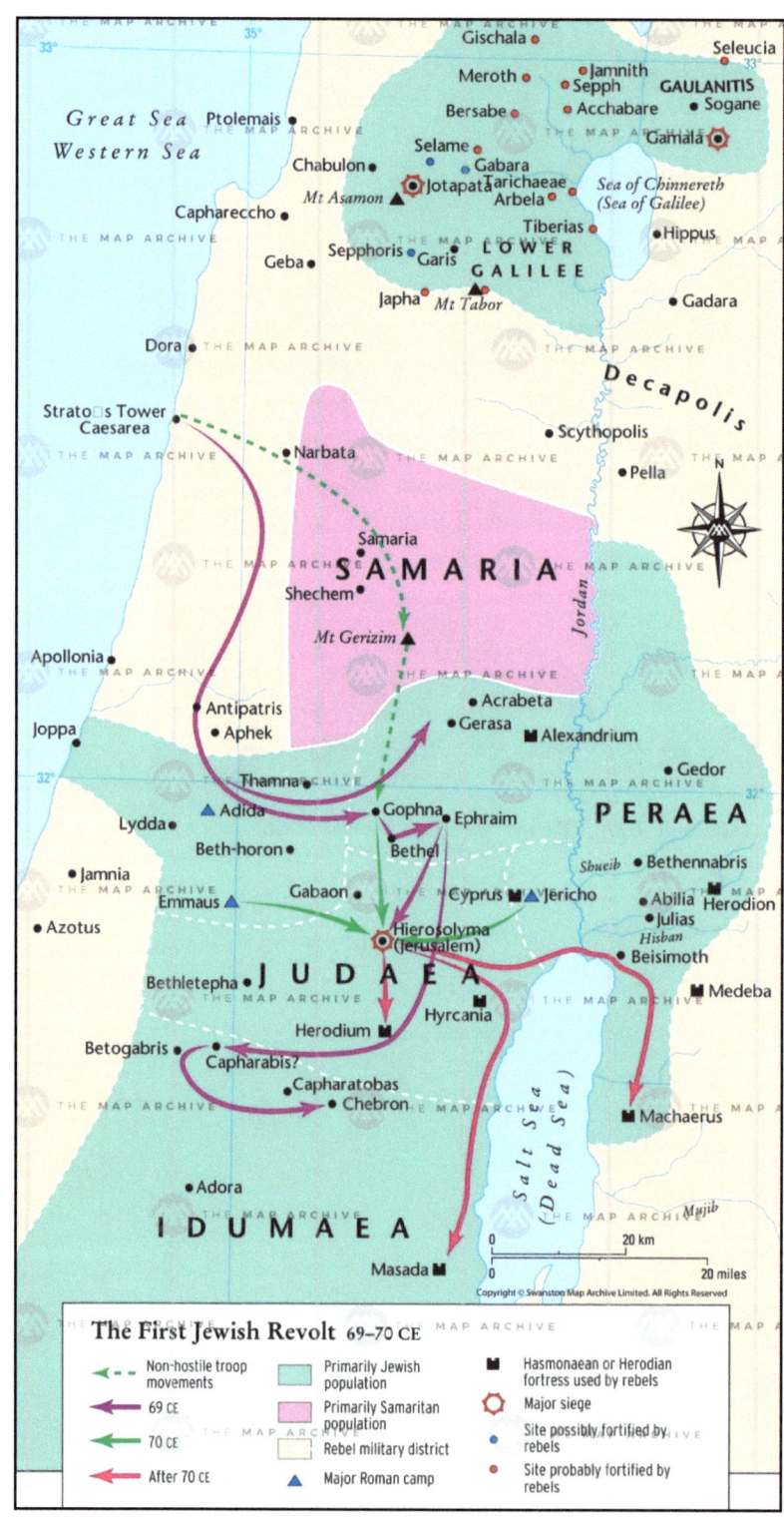

Fig. 34
Map of the last year of the First Revolt, 69-70 CE.

When the Jewish Revolt broke out in 66 CE, the Judaeans quickly captured the holy city of Jerusalem, thus assuring them access to the great Temple for religious purposes and to its vast treasury as well: "Hereupon the soldiers were prevailed upon, and leaped out into the temple, and fought a terrible battle with the Jews ... [and] there were a great many of them destroyed" (*Josephus, Of the War – Book II, 3:2*).

From the silver in the temple, presumably consisting of Tyrian coins paid in taxes over the years, the revolutionaries struck the most famous of all Jewish coins — shekels and half shekels. Quarter shekels were also produced in the first and fourth year of the revolt, but they are extraordinarily rare.

These handsome coins are the first truly Jewish silver coins. They feature a vessel on one side with the year of the revolt above, surrounded by the ancient Hebrew inscription "Shekel of Israel." Three buds are featured on the reverse, with the inscription "Jerusalem the Holy." Just four examples of prototype designs, with a row of dots encircling the symbols, are known.

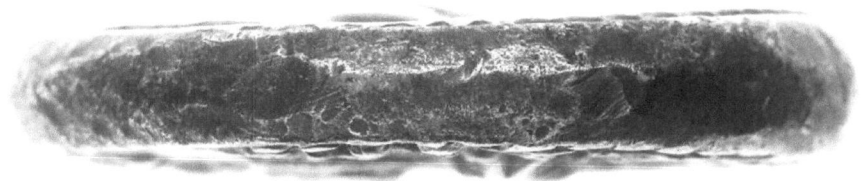

Fig. 35
Hammered edge of a Year 3 half shekel (enlarged). Photo by Lyle Engleson, courtesy of Ira & Larry Goldberg Auctioneers.

Unique in ancient numismatics, the edges of shekels and half shekels were hammered, creating multiple flat facets. David Hendin writes in an auction catalog of the Classical Numismatic Group:

"My examination in hand of three of the four known specimens of the Year 1 prototype show that these examples have the least-hammered edges of the many hundreds of shekels I have closely studied. The Year 1 large chalice shekels show a bit more hammering, while the later Year 1 shekels with the smaller, neater chalice, are almost completely hammered. However, as I noted in *Not Kosher* (New York, 2005), the edges of the Year 1 coins tend toward being flat to slightly rounded while the coins of years two through five are generally hammered both above and below so they have more of a convex edge around the perimeter of the coin. I also note here, for the first time, that I have also examined several shekels of Year 2, which have been hammered in the same way as the later Year 1 coins. This verifies Deutsch's conclusion, and establishes the chronology of manufacturing technique for the

#68
First Revolt, shekel prototype, Year 1 = 66/67 CE (H-1352).

#69
First Revolt, shekel, Year 1 = 66/67 CE (H-1353).

#70
First Revolt, half shekel, Year 1 = 66/67 CE (H-1355).

Mel Wacks 51

#71
First Revolt, quarter shekel,
Year 1 = 66/67 CE (H-1356).

#72
First Revolt, shekel, Year 2
= 67/68 CE (H-1358).

#73
First Revolt, half shekel, Year 2
= 67/68 CE (H-1359).

#74
First Revolt, shekel, Year 3
= 68/69 CE (H-1361).

#75
First Revolt, half shekel, Year 3
= 68/69 CE (H-1362).

#76
First Revolt, shekel, Year 4
= 69/70 CE (H-1364).

Jewish War shekels — first they were struck on un-hammered blanks, then they began to edge-hammer the blanks, and eventually they refined the method to the style used in years two through five.

Regarding the edge hammering, Robert Deutsch (*Jewish Coinage During the First Revolt Against Rome: 66 – 73 CE*, Jaffa, 2018) has noted, '[o]n a number of silver coin-types of Year 1, only partial hammering is evident, and it seems that this treatment only developed as a response to the production of numbers of coins with irregular edges.' Deutsch also observes that 'it seems clear that these edges were hammered as part of the preparation of the blanks, prior to the actual minting … The coin surfaces are flat across their complete area, and hammering the edges after minting would have resulted in a raised rim, as became clear during our trials. The rims on the blanks were flattened out by the force of the hammer-blows during minting'."

Year 1 (66/67 CE) Jewish shekels and half shekels are very scarce, year 2 (67/68 CE) shekels and half shekels are not quite as scarce, year 3 (68/69 CE) shekels and half shekels are very scarce, year 4 (69/70 CE) and year 5 (70 CE) shekels and half shekels are extremely rare. The year 1 and year 4 quarter shekels are exceedingly rare.

Some have called the vessel on the obverse a chalice. But Paul Romanoff (*Jewish Symbols on Ancient Jewish Coins*), writes "It is doubtful whether … the vessel was a drinking cup. The dotted border would make drinking almost impossible … while the drinking of wine in the Temple was forbidden." Romanoff, rather, believes it could be the "golden vessel that contained the omer." On the other hand, Moses ben Nahman (Nachmanides), indicated that he saw "a silver coin engrav[ed with] some sort of dish … [in the] shape [of] the container of manna."

There are also several possible interpretations of the reverse design. Most contemporary reference books call it a budding pomegranate plant — as described in the *Song of Solomon 6:11*: "I went down into the garden of nuts to see the fruits of the valley, and to see whether the vine flourished, and the pomegranates budded," or something else.

In 1864, Federic Madden (*History of Jewish Coinage and of Money in the Old and New Testament*) described the reverse motif as "a triple lily," but by 1881 Madden (in *Coins of the Jews*) had changed his mind — calling it "?Aaron's rod." This attribution has been reinforced recently by Robert Deutsch (*The Jewish Revolt against Rome, Interdisciplinary Perspectives — Coinage of the First Jewish*

Revolt against Rome: Iconography, Minting Authority, Metallurgy, Brill, 2011). Deutsch writes that "The only symbol on the coins for which we had no straightforward explanation was the rod with three ... buds. If the assumption that this is a staff is correct, then it may be identified with the Jewish high priest": "And on the following day Moses came to the Tent of Testimony, and behold, Aaron's staff for the house of Levi had blossomed! It gave forth blossoms, sprouted buds, and produced ripe almonds" (*Numbers 17:23*).

#77
*First Revolt, half shekel, Year 4
= 69/70 CE (H-1365).*

The two sides of the Shekel could well illustrate what Maimonides described: "When [King Solomon] constructed the [Temple in Jerusalem] ... Together with [the ark], were entombed Aaron's staff, the vial [of manna], and the anointing oil." (*Hilchos Beis HaBechirah, Chapter 4*).

#78
*First Revolt, quarter shekel, Year 4
= 69/70 CE (H-1366).*

This explanation of the shekel motifs would also jibe with the writings of the great rabbi Moses ben Nahman (Nachmanides), 1194-1270, who sent the following additions to his commentaries, after visiting Eretz Israel:

"The Lord has blessed me so greatly, for I have been so fortunate as to come to Acco and there to find in the hands of the elders of the land a silver coin with engravings, on one side resembling the branch of an almond tree, on the other some sort of dish ... [The Samaritans] say that the shapes are Aaron's staff, with its almonds and blossoms, and the other shape, the container of manna."

#79
*First Revolt, shekel, Year 5
= 70 CE (H-1370).*

#80
*First Revolt, half shekel, Year 5
= 70 CE (H-1371).*

Bronze prutot were issued in the second and third years of the revolt. They feature an amphora (uncovered on year 2, and a pointed cover on year 3), with the date and poignant Hebrew inscription "The Deliverance of Zion."

#81
*First Revolt, prutah, Year 2
= 67/68 CE (H-1360).*

There are also three sizes of larger bronze coins, minted in the fourth year of the revolt, presumably when the supply of silver was running low. The smallest does not have a denomination indicated, but is usually referred to as an eighth? [shekel]. It is assumed that all of these denominations are fractions of a shekel. Like the silver coins, a vessel is featured, along with symbols of the harvest festival of Succoth — lulav (bunch of branches) and etrog (lime-like fruit). The date and inscription "For the Redemption of Zion" is inscribed.

#82
*First Revolt, prutah, Year 3
= 68/69 CE (H-1363).*

Mel Wacks 53

#83
*First Revolt, [eighth? shekel],
Year 4 = 69/70 CE (H-1369).*

#84
*First Revolt, quarter [shekel],
Year 4 = 69/70 CE (H-1368).*

#85
*First Revolt, half [shekel], Year 4
= 69/70 CE (H-1367).*

The medium bronze has the same inscription, with the denomination "reva" (quarter [shekel]) indicated; a large etrog is depicted on the obverse, and two lulav are shown on the reverse. The largest bronze coins are inscribed "chatzi" (half) [shekel]; again the lulav and etrog are pictured on one side, with a palm tree and baskets on the reverse.

*Fig. 36
Lulav and etrog are pictured
In Prayer at Sukkot, painting
by Paula Gans, 1920.*

Lastly, there were extraordinary coins issued during the First Revolt, that were unknown until recent years, when 7 examples were discovered in an excavation at Gamla, located in the center of what is now the Golan Heights.

Flavius Josephus (*The Jewish War*, translated by H. S.. Thackery) told of the final hours of the defenders of Gamla: "Despairing of their lives and hemmed in on every side, multitudes plunged headlong with their wives and children into the ravine which had been excavated to a vast depth beneath the citadel. Indeed, the rage of the Romans was thus made to appear milder than the frantic self-immolation of the vanquished, four thousand only being slain by the former, while those who flung themselves over the cliff were found to exceed five thousand … the rage of the Romans was such that they spared not even infants, but time after time snatched up numbers of them and slung them from the citadel.

*#86
First Revolt, mint of Gamla,
66/67 CE (H-1372).*

Thus, on the twenty-third of the month Hyperberetaeus [October 20, 67 CE] was Gamla taken, after a revolt which began on the twenty-fourth of Gorpiaeus [August]."

Shekels must have been made shortly after the First Revolt broke out, since just about a month later, crude bronze coins mimicking the chalice on the silver Shekels minted in Jerusalem, were being produced in Gamla. These crude coins were probably minted during the 47 days of siege.

The Gamla bronze coins are so crude that modern numismatic scholars cannot agree on the inscriptions; they can't even agree whether they are written in Paleo-Hebrew or Aramaic. For the obverse, Meshorer translates as "for the redemption of," while Farhi interprets it as either "Gamla [year] 2" or "to the freedom." For the reverse, Meshorer translates as "ho[ly] Jerusalem," while Farhi believes it is "y[ear] the Jewish People."

Judaea Capta

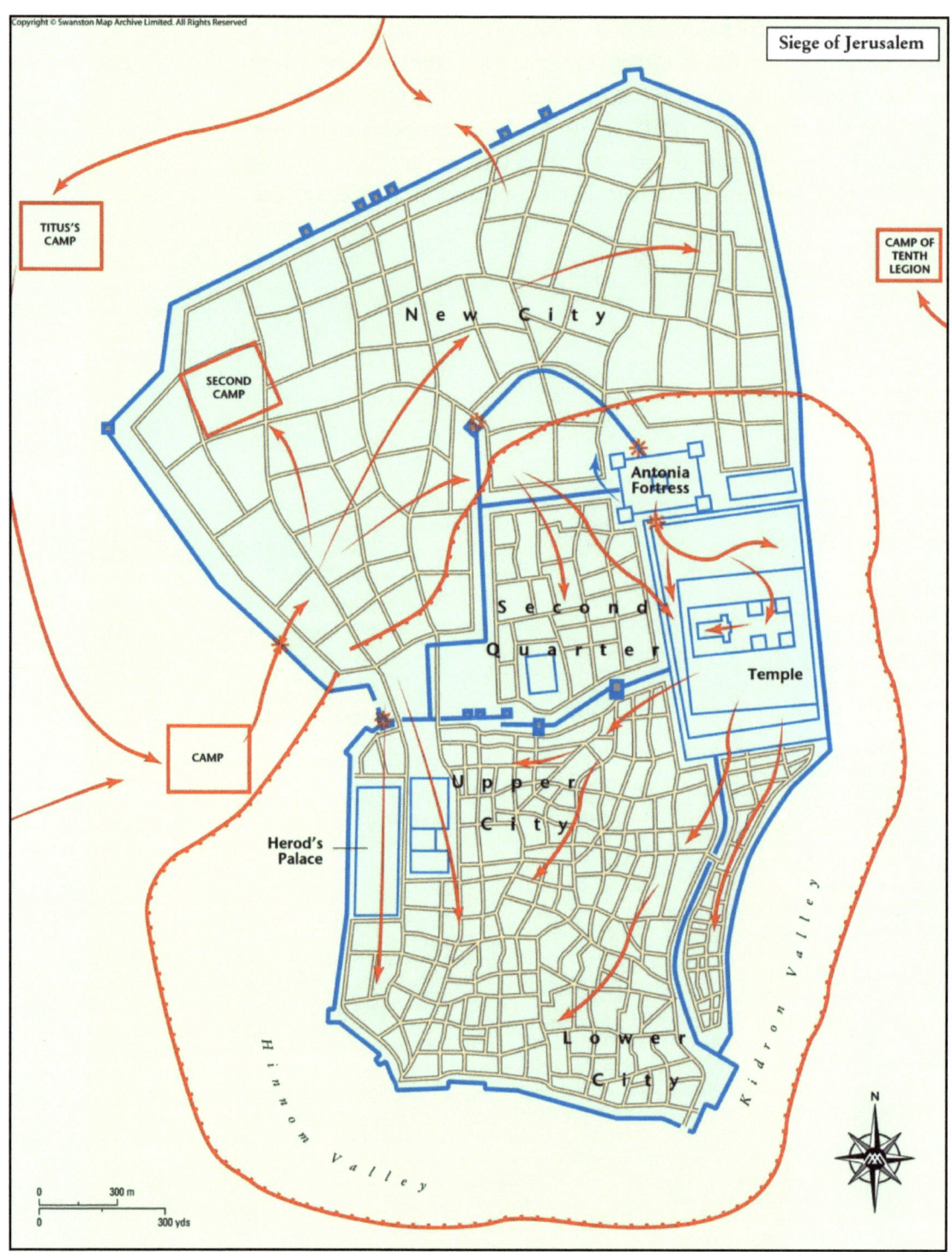

Fig. 37
Map of the siege of Jerusalem, 70 CE. Courtesy of The Map Archive.

Soon after the Temple at Jerusalem was razed by the victorious troops led by Titus in 70 CE, his father — Emperor Titus Flavius Vespasian — launched an extensive issue of coins commemorating the hard fought Roman victory over the tiny Jewish nation. The Judaea Capta series lasted for 25 years under Vespasian and his two sons who succeeded him as Emperor — Titus and Domitian. These commemoratives were issued in bronze, silver and gold by mints in Rome, the Roman Empire, and Judaea.

The basic design elements of the coins struck in Rome or in its Empire are a palm tree and a seated figure of a female (allegorical representative of Judaea) in an attitude of mourning. The depiction on these coins may reflect the prophesy of Isaiah (c. 700 BCE): "For Jerusalem is ruined, and Judah is fallen ... Thy men shall fall by the sword and thy mighty in the war. And her gates shall lament and mourn, and she being desolate shall sit upon the ground" (*Isaiah 3:8, 25-26*). Other Judaea Capta varieties include the standing figure of the victorious emperor, a male captive, the goddess Victory, and Roman symbols of war.

The most common Judaea Capta coin is the silver denarius issued by Vespasian, picturing Judaea weeping beneath a Roman trophy, and the inscription IVDAEA. Other denarii of Vespasian show Judaea seated next to a palm tree, Judaea standing next to a palm tree with her hands bound, inscribed IVDAEA DEVICTA, a tiny Jewish captive next to Victory, Judaea seated beneath a palm tree with a Roman soldier standing alongside, etc. Some of these designs also appeared on gold coins.

#87
Vespasian, denarius, 70/71 CE (H-1479).

#88
Vespasian, denarius, 70/71 CE (H-1488).

#89
Vespasian, denarius, 75/76 CE (H-1485).

#90
Vespasian, denarius, 72/73 CE (H-1490).

#91
Vespasian, aureus, 70/71 CE (H-1465).

#92
Vespasian, aureus, 70/71 CE (H-1464).

Mel Wacks

The large bronze sestertius and medium as denominations comes in many variations, with captive females, males, the goddess Victory, and the Roman Emperor in various combinations.

#93
Vespasian, sestertius, 71 CE (H-1504).

#94
Vespasian, sestertius, 71 CE (H-1508).

#95
Vespasian, as, mint of Lyon
(Lugdunum), 77/78 CE (H-1561).

#96
Titus, sestertius, 80/81 CE (H-1596a).

Small bronze Judaea Capta quadrans and semis coins were also struck.

#97
Vespasian, quadrans, 72/73 CE (H-1571).

#98
Titus, semis, 80/81 CE (H-1598a).

Bronze Judaea Capta coins were also struck in Caesarea, in the defeated Roman province of Judaea. These are cruder than the Roman issues, and the inscriptions are in Greek rather than Latin. Designs feature the goddess Nike writing on a shield, Minerva with a trophy, a palm tree, etc. Most were issued during the reign of the Emperor Domitian (81-96 CE).

David Hendin writes (*Echoes of "Judaea Capta,"* Israel Numismatic Journal, 2007): "While these coins do not carry JUDAEA CAPTA legends, the population was by any account largely illiterate. Images must have spoken louder than words in conveying the 'Judaea Capta' message during the two decades that followed issue of the explicit local 'Judaea Capta' coins of Vespasian and Titus."

#99
Titus, 70-81 CE (H-1446).

#100
Domitian, c. 83 CE or later (H-1455).

#101
Domitian, 92/93 CE (H-1458).

Nerva Reforms Jewish Tax

In 70 CE, after the fall of Jerusalem, many thousands of Jews were taken to Rome as slaves and others were exiled from Judaea. Rome took over the collection of the annual Jewish head tax, which had been a half shekel (equivalent to two Roman denarii). The Romans collected this tax with much zeal — so much so that it caused embarrassment to Jews and non-Jews alike. The historian Suetonius wrote (*Domitian 12.1–2*) that victims of the tax were non-Jews who "lived a Jewish life without publicly acknowledging that fact" [i.e. Jewish sympathizers and gentile Christians] and Jews who "concealed their origin and did not pay the tribute levied upon their people [i.e. apostate Jews and Jewish Christians]."

Following the reign of the Flavians — Vespasian, Titus and Domitian — came the short but liberalizing rule of Marcus Nerva (96-98 CE). One of the first reforms he instituted concerned the department (Fiscus Judaicus) responsible for the collection of the Jewish head tax.

#102A
Nerva, sestertius, COS II = 96 CE (H-1603a).

A large bronze sestertius was issued to commemorate this reform. This scarce coin features a palm tree, that had become symbolic of the Jewish people on the Judaea Capta coins, and the Latin inscriptions "FISCI IVDAICI CALVMNIA SVBLATA" (the calumny of the Jewish tax is removed) and "S C" (by consent of the Senate).

#102B
Nerva, sestertius, COS III = 97 CE (H-1603b).

Fisci Judaici sestertii were initially issued in 96 CE, with the obverse inscription of IMP NERVA CAES AVG P M TR COS II DESIGN III P P, The following year, it was changed to IMP NERVA CAES AVG P M TR P COS III P P. "COS II" or "III" indicates that the coin was issued in the second or third year of Nerva's consulship. David Hendin (*Guide to Biblical Coins*) indicates that there are also Fisci Judaici sestertitii dated "COS IIII, but I haven't been able to confirm this.

In imperial times the consulship became the senior administrative office under the emperors, who frequently assumed the title of consul themselves. "DESIGN" meant that the person had been designated as consul for the following year.

One theory espoused that these coins commemorated the abolition of the tax. Later, it was postulated that this coin commemorated the end of the insulting methods of collecting the tax, which had demanded visible (and public) proof of circumcision. In Marius Heemstra's paper *The Interpretation and Wider Context of Nerva's Fiscus Judaicus Sestertius*, presented at the International Conference Judaea and Rome in Coins in 2010, she came to the conclusion that "Nerva's coin … is very plausibly evidence that the new emperor no longer permitted people to be accused of living a Jewish life. This specific accusation became a 'wrongful accusation' (calumnia). Towards the end of [his predecessor] Domitian's reign, high-ranking Romans accused of 'living a Jewish life' could have their property confiscated and they could even end up being executed."

The Kitos War

Fig. 38
Map of the Roman Empire, c. 117 CE.

The First Revolt took place from 66-70 CE, and the so-called Second Revolt, led by Bar Kochba, lasted from 132-135 CE. However, another Jewish uprising took place 115-117 CE, mainly among the Jewish diaspora in the Roman provinces during the reign of the Emperor Trajan. It is called the "Kitos War," after the Roman general Lusius Quietus ("Kitos" being a later corruption of "Quietus").

Roman General Lusius Quietus was commander of the Moorish cavalry in the Roman army that subdued the Jewish revolt in Mesopotamia. As a reward for his success in military campaigns, Quietus was appointed governor of Judaea in 117 CE by Trajan (Eusebius, *Historia Ecclesiastica*, 4:2).

Quietus laid siege to Lydda (now Lod), where the Jews had gathered.

When Lydda was taken, mass numbers of Jews were executed. The "slain of Lydda" are often mentioned in words of reverential praise in the Talmud (Pes. 50a; B. B. 10b; Eccl. R. ix. 10).

Fig. 39
Stylized Berber Cavalry under Lusius Quietus, fighting against the Dacians. From the Column of Trajan.

Soon after Trajan died, Lusius Quietus was recalled by the new Emperor Hadrian and executed shortly afterward as a possible rival (*Spartianus, "Vita Hadriani," §§ 5, 7; Dio Cassius, lxix*).

While there aren't any coins to memorialize this Jewish revolt, Trajan did issue coins struck in Palestine during Trajan's rule, while the Kitos War was taking place.

#103
Ascalon, Trajan, 116/117 CE.

Hadrian's Trip to Judaea

Fig. 40
Map showing the travels of the Emperor Hadrian, 121-132 CE. Courtesy of The Map Archive.

The Roman Emperor Publius Aelius Hadrian (117-138 CE) visited many of the Roman provinces, including Judaea in 130 CE. Immediately, the rumor spread among the Jewish inhabitants that the Emperor, one of the great ancient builders, intended to rebuild the Jewish Temple in Jerusalem. He did intend to build a temple on this holy site — but it was to be a pagan Roman temple dedicated to the god Jupiter (Zeus). Leo Kadman writes: "The Jews watched the stones of the Sanctuary being used to erect temples for heathen gods. No choice was left to them but to interrupt the building of the Roman colony by force of arms before it was completed" (*The Coins of Aelia Capitolina*).

At the age of 60, Hadrian returned to Rome from his travels, and began to strike coins to commemorate his visits to the empire's provinces — Egypt, Macedonia, Spain, etc. — and the Judaean visit was no exception. His ADVENTVI AVG IVDAEAE bronze sestertius shows the Emperor receiving a Jewish woman and two children who carry palm branches; in the background, a bull appears next to a sacrificial altar. The altar was a reference to the god Jupiter Capitolinus, to whom Hadrian had dedicated his new pagan temple. Hadrian renamed Jerusalem as Aelia (his family name) Capitolina.

Hadrian issued a couple of other coin-types commemorating his trip to Judaea.

#104
Hadrian, sestertius, c. 134-138 CE (H-1604).

#105
Hadrian, sestertius, c. 134-138 CE (H-1605).
© The Trustees of the British Museum.

The Second Revolt

Fig. 41
Map of the Bar Kochba Revolt, 132-135 CE. Courtesy of The Map Archive.

The leader of the Second Revolt (132-135 CE) was Shim'on Bar Koseba. He was known as Bar Kochba, meaning "Son of the Star," in reference to messianic expectations of the verse: "There shall step forth a star (kochab) out of Jacob" (*Numbers 24:17*). Indeed, one of the greatest sages of the time — Rabbi Akiva — had proclaimed Bar Kochba as the messiah.

The authors of the Babylonian Talmud (c. 350 CE) were well aware of the Judaean coins minted for both the First and Second Revolts, as can be seen in: "Bet Hillel says: a shekel of silver and a shekel's worth of copper coins [can be exchanged for the sela]" (Mishnah Maaser Sheni). And in: "The rabbis taught: If there are three who have qualified as a Beth Din [rabbinical court]... if one appraises the estate at one hundred zuz, which are twenty-five selas, the second for twenty, and the third for thirty, the value is fixed at one hundred zuz" (Tractate Baba Bathra). Indeed, four zuzim have the value of a sela. Modern numismatists do not know the names of the denominations of Bar Kochba's bronze coins, and just describe them by size — small, medium and large (or Abu Jara, an Arabic word).

A few coin-types were issued at the beginning of the revolt with the name "Eleazar the Priest (Cohen)," who may have been Bar Kochba's uncle or perhaps it was a "messianic and heroic reference to Eleazar the Priest, son of Aaron, whose name was known to every Jew of the time," as proposed by David Hendin.

#106
Second Revolt, "Eleazar the Priest," zuz, Year 1 = 132/133 CE (H-1374).

Unlike the situation at the start of the First Revolt, in Bar Kochba's time there was no Temple and no Temple Treasury. So, in order to mint their own coins as a sign of sovereignty, they gathered all of the bronze and silver foreign (Rome, Syria, Phoenicia, etc.) coins circulating in Judaea. Then they filed off the original designs and restamped them with Jewish symbols and Hebrew inscriptions relating to their hope of rebuilding the Temple. Many coins exhibit parts of the original designs and legends. Coins minted in the first two years are dated Year 1 and Year 2 "of the Freedom (or Redemption) of Israel (or Jerusalem)." But in the third year, when the revolt became more of a defensive guerrilla action, the inscription changed to the hope "For the Freedom of Jerusalem."

#107
Second Revolt, "Eleazar the Priest," small bronze, Year 1 = 132/133 CE (H-1380).

The overstruck silver tetradrachms (called "sela'im" in the Mishnah) are among the most religiously significant coins issued by the ancient Jews. They depict the Holy of Holies within the Jerusalem Temple, along with the Ark — that purportedly held the two tablets of the Ten Commandments. "Jerusalem" was inscribed around the Temple in the first year and on some very rare sela'im of the second year. A discussion of all other obverse design elements can be found in Appendix B.

Mel Wacks 67

#108
Second Revolt, "Jerusalem," sela,
Year 1 = 132/133 CE (H-1373).

Agricultural symbols associated with the harvest festival of Succoth — lulav and etrog — appear on the reverse of the sela, surrounded by a Hebrew inscription: "Year One of the Redemption of Israel," "Year Two of the Freedom of Israel," or "For the Freedom of Jerusalem," respectively in the three years of the revolt.

In a letter from Bar Kochba, discovered in the late 1950s, the Jewish leader orders Judah Ben Manasseh to supply him with lulav for his army so that they could celebrate the festival even though they were in the midst of major battles: **"And you shall take for yourselves on the first day [of the Festival of Succoth], the fruit of the hadar tree, date palm fronds, a branch of a braided tree, and willows of the brook, and you shall rejoice before the Lord your God for a seven day period"** (*Lev. 23:40*).

#109
Second Revolt, "Shim'on," sela,
Year 2 = 133/134 CE (H-1388).

#110
Second Revolt, "Shim'on," sela,
Year 2 = 134/135 CE (H-1411).

#111
Second Revolt, "Shim'on," sela,
Year 3 = 134/135 CE (H-1413).

#112
Second Revolt, "Shim'o," zuz,
Year 2 = 133/134 CE (H-1392).

There are dozens of varieties of overstruck Roman silver denarii (called "zuz" in Hebrew). Some very rare Year 1 zuzim are inscribed Eleazar the Priest instead of Shim'on. Otherwise, most have an abbreviated form of Bar Kochba's first name "Shim'o" or the full name "Shim'on" within a wreath on one side, and the date (Year 1 or 2) or "For the Freedom of Jerusalem" (Year 3) on the reverse. The symbols are associated with the Temple — palm branch, amphora, bunch of grapes, lyre and trumpets.

#113
Second Revolt, "Shim'on," zuz,
Year 2 = 133/134 CE (H-1393).

"All the Levites who were musicians — Asaph, Heman, Jeduthun and their sons and relatives — stood on the east side of the altar, dressed in fine linen and playing cymbals, harps and lyres. They were accompanied by 120 priests sounding trumpets" (*2 Chronicles 5:12*).

Shim'o could also have been a rallying cry, since it is also the first word in the Jewish Prayer that is the centerpiece of the daily morning and evening prayer services and is considered by some the most essential prayer in all of Judaism. An affirmation of God's singularity and kingship, its daily recitation is regarded as a biblical commandment: "Hear, O Israel: The Lord is our God; the Lord is one" (*Deuteronomy 6:4*).

#114
Second Revolt, "Shim'on," zuz,
Year 3 = 134/135 CE (H-1430).
Clearly struck over portrait of Emperor Titus on Roman denarius, 79-81 CE.

The rarest of all Bar Kochba denominations is the large bronze, overstruck (often weak, with parts of the design or inscription indistinct) on a Roman sestertius. These coins are known by the Arabic nickname "Abu Jara," meaning "father of the jar." The obverse is inscribed "Shim'on" or "Jerusalem" within a wreath, while the reverse features an amphora — which Romanoff concludes "was the vessel of oil which nourished the flames of the Temple Menorah."

#115
Second Revolt, "Jerusalem," Abu Jara,
Year 1 = 133/134 CE (H-1375).

A file was used to remove the designs of the underlying coins, and this is often apparent on some of the large bronzes.

#116
Second Revolt, "Shim'on," Abu Jara,
Year 2 = 133/134 CE (H-1405).

Some of the medium bronzes of Bar Kochba picture a grape vine leaf and 7-branched palm tree. The seven branches of the palm tree could well allude to the holy 7-branched Temple Menorah, that was considered too holy to depict on coins (with the isolated exception of the small bronze Menorah coin issued in the last desperate days of the reign of Mattathias Antigonus). Bar Kochba's given name appears on the palm tree side either in full with his title: Shim'on Nasi (leader) of Israel, or without the title: Shim'on, or abbreviated to Shim'o.

#117
Second Revolt, "Shim'on Nasi of Israel," middle bronze,
Year 1 = 132/133 CE (H-1378).

#118
Second Revolt, "Shim'on, middle bronze,
Year 2 = 133/134 CE (H-1408a).

#119
Second Revolt, "Shim'on (misspelled), middle bronze, Year 2 = 133/134 CE (H-1408a).

#120
Second Revolt, "Shim'on Prince of Israel," middle bronze, Year 1 = 132/133 CE (H-1377).

Other middle bronzes of Bar Kochba feature an upright palm branch within a wreath, and a lyre. The lyre is either a wide 4-6 stringed chelys type or narrow 3 stringed kithara. The Jewish leader's name and title surround the wreath: "Shim'on Prince of Israel," while a patriotic (and religiously significant) motto is inscribed on the reverse, such as "Year One of the Redemption of Israel," "Year Two of the Freedom of Jerusalem," or "For the Freedom of Jerusalem."

#121
Second Revolt,"For the Freedom of Jerusalem," middle bronze, Year 3 = 134/135 CE (H-1436).

#122
Second Revolt, "Jerusalem," small bronze, Year 2 = 133/134 CE (H-1410).

The small bronze coins issued during the Second Revolt all picture a bunch of grapes, and a 7-branched palm tree with clusters of dates. The legends surrounding the grapes are similar to other issues: "Year One of the Redemption of Israel," "Year Two of the Freedom of Jerusalem," "For the Freedom of Jerusalem," etc. The inscription around the palm tree begins in the first year with "Eleazar the Priest" and changes to "Jerusalem," which continues through the second year, and finally changes to "Shim'on" in the third year of the revolt.

It is estimated that over half a million Jews fell in battle during the Second Revolt, with countless more sold as slaves after the final defeat of Bar Kochba at Betar. The Romans too suffered such heavy losses that when Hadrian sent a written report of the campaign to the senate, he omitted the usual introductory remarks that the emperor and the army were well.

#123
Second Revolt, "Shim'on," small bronze, Year 3 = 134/135 CE (H-1440).

The coins issued by Bar Kochba marked the last coins issued by an autonomous Jewish State until the establishment of Israel in 1948.

However, many of the Second Revolt coins had a second life! A number of Second Revolt silver zuzim have been discovered with holes drilled through them, but these perforations never obliterated the meaningful designs.

Holed Bar Kochba coins were discussed in the Mishnah (written before 200 CE): "A denarius which was invalidated and fashioned for hanging around the neck of a young girl is susceptible to uncleanliness" (*Kelim 12, 7*). And again, there is a reference in the Jerusalem Talmud: "With regard to a coin which was invalidated ... the second tithe is not exchanged for a coin issued by one who rebelled, such as Ben Kosiva [Bar Koseva]" (*Ma'aser Sheni 1, 2*).

Thus, it can be concluded that after the beautiful zuzim of Bar Kochba became worthless as money, people chose to wear them as jewelry, proudly and defiantly displaying the symbols associated with the Second Temple period.

#124
Second Revolt, perforated, zuz, Year 3 = 134/5 CE.

#125
Second Revolt, perforated, zuz, Year 3 = 134/5 CE.

City Coins of Palestine

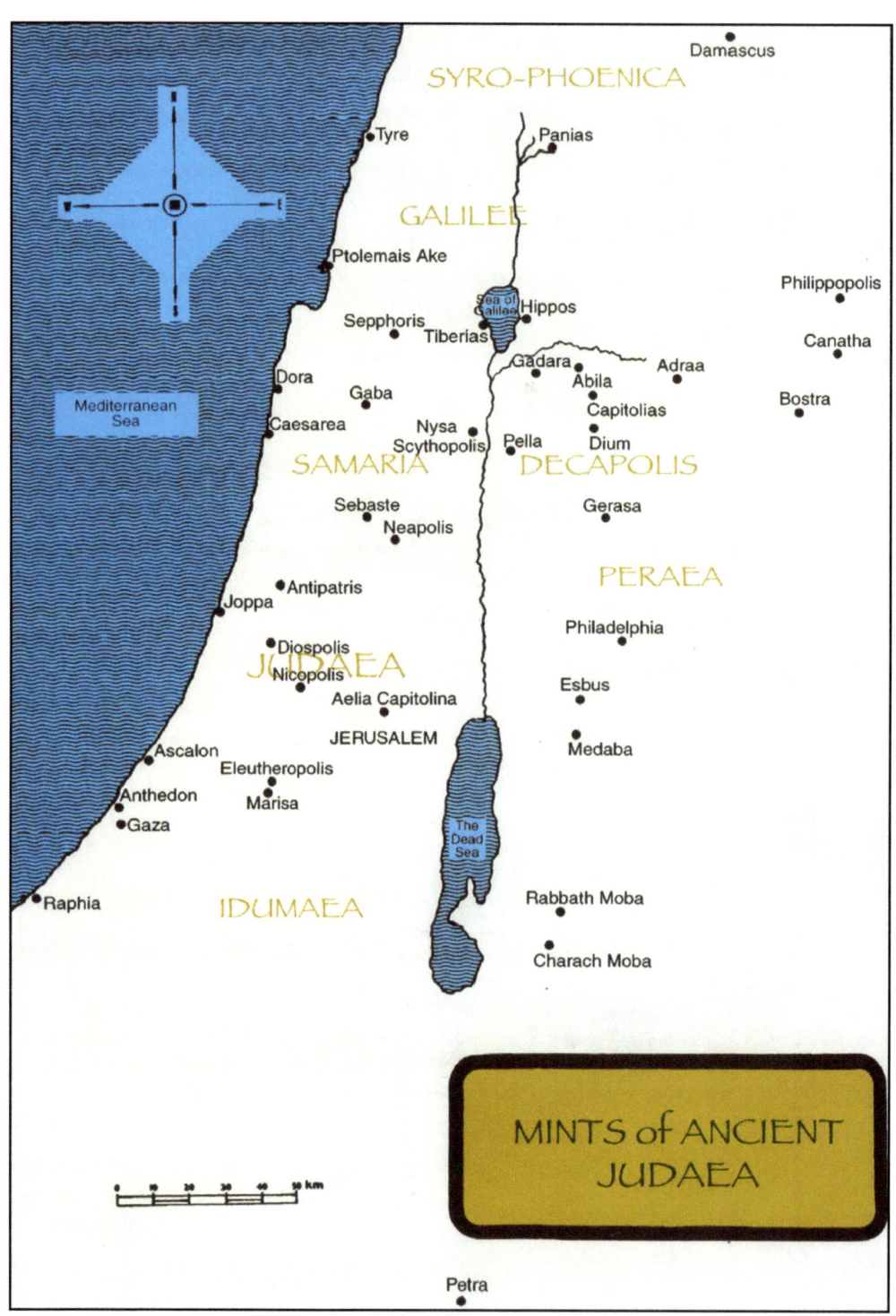

Fig. 42
Map showing the mints of ancient Judaea. Courtesy of David Hendin.

In the first century CE, the Roman Empire granted many of the cities in its provinces the right to mint bronze coins. Silver coins were only minted in a few important cities outside of Rome. According to Ya'akov Meshorer, coins were issued in Judaea/Palestine by the following cities, listed from north to south:

Coastal Cities:

Ptolemais (Akko)
Dora (Dor)
Caesarea
Joppa (Yafo)
Ascalon (Ashkelon)
Gaza
Anthedon
Raphia

Inland Cities:

Tiberias
Sepphoris (Sippori)
Gaba
Nysa-Scythopolis
Samaria (Shomron-Sebaste)
Neapolis (Shechem)
Antipatris
Diospolis (Lod)
Nicopolis (Emmaus)
Aelia Capitolina (Jerusalem)
Eleutheropolis (Beth Govrin)

Cities of Transjordan:

Panias
Philippopolis
Hippos (Susita)
Canatha (Kenath)
Abilla (Abel)
Gadara (Gader)
Adraa
Capitolias (Beth Reisha)
Bostra (Beser)
Dium
Pella (Pehal)
Gerasa (Geresh)
Philadelphia (Rabbat Ammon)
Esbus (Heshbon)
Medeba
Rabbath-Moba (Rabbath Moab)
Charach-Moba (Kir Moab)
Petra (Reqem)

The definition of "Palestinian" cities is somewhat subjective. The British Museum Catalog of Palestine coins tallies 16 cities in Galilee, Samaria and Judaea; Klimowsky lists 32 cities under the heading "Palestine;" and Rosenberger enumerates 22 cities in "Palestine" and 18 in "Eastern Palestine."

While a scattering of city coins were minted earlier, the time of the First Revolt (66-70 CE) saw the initial widespread production of city coins in Judaea — and the number of mints blossomed after the defeat of the Jews in the Second Revolt (132-135 CE). The Ascalon Mint deserves special mention, since it produced coins almost continuously from about 375 BCE through 235 CE; one of its more interesting issues features the famous Cleopatra on a silver shekel.

#126
Ascalon, with Cleopatra VII, shekel, 47 BCE.

#127
Neapolis, with Domitian, 82/83 CE.

A few cities, with large Jewish populations — Neapolis and Sepphoris — initially struck coins with Jewish symbols.

#128
Sepphoris, with Trajan, 98-117 CE.

#129
Aelia Capitolina, with Hadrian, 130 CE (H-Fig. 10.1).

Some coins — issued by Aelia Capitolina/Jerusalem, Caesarea, etc. — picture the Roman ceremonial founding of the city. The Emperor is shown in a cart pulled by a bull and ox, defining the boundary as the area enclosed by a plough in 24 hours.

#130
Caesarea Maritima, with Septimus Severus 193-211 CE.

#131
Neapolis, Samaria, with Otacilia Severa, wife of Philip I, and Mount Gerizim, 244-249 CE.

But the coins of these cities eventually joined with the others in depicting Roman gods, goddesses, temples, etc. One of the most interesting designs depicts a Roman temple, dedicated to the worship of Jupiter, which was erected on the former site of the Samaritan Temple atop Mt. Gerizim. The Samaritan temple was referred to when: **"Then cometh he [Jesus] to a city of Samaria ... The woman saith unto him ... Our fathers worshipped in this mountain, and ye say, that in Jerusalem is the place where men ought to worship"** *(John 4:5, 19-20).*

One coin even features a zodiac. But this is not antithetic to Jewish views, since the mystical teachings of the Zohar, written in the 2nd century CE, correlates the 12 signs of the zodiac to the 12 Hebrew months and the 12 tribes of Israel (I:173).

This extensive series of Palestine city-coins finally came to an end during the reign of Gallienus (253-268 CE).

#132
Akko-Ptolemais, with Salonina,
wife of Galienus, 253-268 CE.
Courtesy of the Israel Museum. Gift
of Abraham & Marian Sofaer
in honor of Dr. Ya'akov Meshorer.

Scenes from the Bible

Fig. 43
Map showing the location of Apameia Kibotos, after third century BCE.

Apameia Kibotos was a Phrygian city (currently in Turkey) established by Antiochus I (280–261 BCE), who named it after his mother Apameia. Part of its name, "Kibotos," means both "chest" and "ark" in Greek. Apamea also seems to have had a strong Jewish presence, as Josephus describes how the Seleucid king Antiochus III **"brought Babylonian Jews to Phrygia to serve as garrison soldiers, civil servants and royal administrators in the newly established city"** (*Antiquities, 12.3.4*). There was a local tradition that the nearby mountain was in fact Mount Ararat:

"There is in Phrygia on the dark mainland
A steep, tall mountain; Ararat its name …
There on a lofty peak the ark abode
When the waters ceased, and then again from heaven
The voice divine of the great God this word
Proclaimed: "O Noah, guarded, faithful, just,
Come boldly forth, with thy sons and thy wife
And the three brides, and fill ye all the earth"
(*The Sibylline Oracles, 1.320-334*).

Coins depicting Noah and a chest-shaped ark were issued under Roman Emperors Severus Alexander (222-235 CE), Gordian III (238-234 CE), Philip I (244-249 CE), and Trebonianus Gallus (251-253 CE). The basic design features Noah, with his name "NΩE" on the ark. Noah and his wife standing to the left or right, and are also shown in a square chest (the ark) on the right; a dove perches on the ark and another dove flies above, holding an olive branch.

#133
Apameia Kibotos, with Septimus Severus, 193-211 CE.

These coins depict the events described in the Old Testament: "And the dove returned to him at eventide, and behold it had plucked an olive leaf in its mouth; so Noah knew that the water had abated from upon the earth" (*Genesis 8:11*).

#134
Apameia Kibotos, with Trebonianus Gallus, 251–253 CE. Courtesy of the Israel Museum. Gift of Abraham & Marian Sofaer in honor of Dr. Ya'akov Meshorer.

Fig. 44
A box-like ark, as depicted on the coins of Apameia Kibotos, in the Roman Catacombs of Marcellinus and Peter, a massive 2nd-3rd century funeral complex.

Another coin depicting a Biblical scene pictures the Old Testament story of the Binding of Isaac: "And they came to the place of which God had spoken to him, and Abraham built the altar there and arranged the wood, and he bound Isaac his son and placed him on the altar upon the wood. And Abraham stretched forth his hand and took the knife, to slaughter his son ... And [God] said, "Do not stretch forth your hand to the lad, nor do the slightest thing to him, for now I know that you are a God fearing man, and you did not withhold your son, your only one, from Me. And Abraham lifted up his eyes, and he saw, and lo! there

#135
Neapolis, with Philip I and Philip II, 247–249 CE. Courtesy of the Israel Museum. Gift of Abraham & Marian Sofaer in honor of Dr. Ya'akov Meshorer.

Mel Wacks 77

was a ram, [and] after [that] it was caught in a tree by its horns. And Abraham went and took the ram and offered it up as a burnt offering instead of his son" (*Genesis 8: 9, 10, 12, 13*).

Neapolis was founded by Vespasian in 72/73 CE, soon after the end of the First Revolt. Located in Samaria, it was originally the home of a Samaritan temple atop Mt. Gerizim. Later, a Roman temple was built by Hadrian on the ancient sacred site that was described in *Deuteronomy 27:11-12*: "And Moses commanded the people on that day, saying, When you cross the Jordan, the following shall stand upon Mount Gerizim to bless the people: Simeon, Levi, Judah, Issachar, Joseph, and Benjamin." Hadrian's temple, dedicated to Zeus, was intended to replace the Jewish Temple in Jerusalem, that had been destroyed a few years earlier. It can be seen in the background of the "Binding of Isaac" coin.

Islamic Coins Inspired by Ancient Judaean Coins

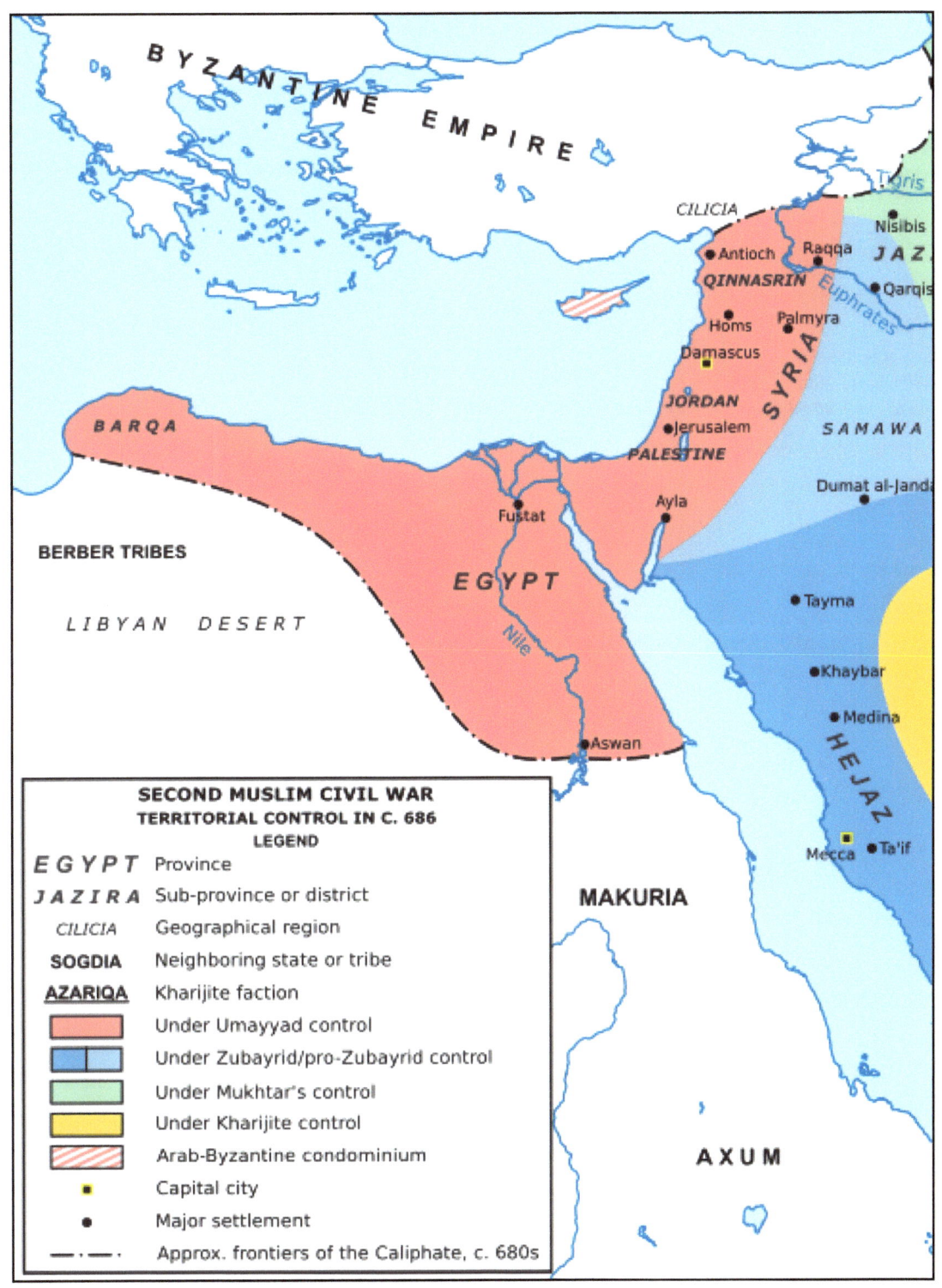

Fig. 45
Map of the Umayyad Caliphate, c. 686 CE.

The Roman Emperor Heraclius lost Jerusalem to the Arabian Khalif Omar in 637 CE, after a few month's siege. The Umayyad Governors struck several varieties of small bronze coins (fals denomination) in imitation of earlier Judaean coins.

These coins feature an amphora (like the design on the prefect Gratus' bronze prutah), a 5-branched candelabrum (similar to the 7-branched Menorah coin of Mattathias Antigonus), and a bud (like the buds on the famous First Revolt shekels). The Arabic inscriptions read "There is No God but Allah Alone" and "Muhammad is the Apostle of Allah." Some speculate that these coins may have been made for the Jewish population of Jerusalem.

#136
Jerusalem?, anonymous fals, after 696 CE. Similar to prefect Valerius Gratus prutah (17/18 CE).

#137
Jerusalem?, anonymous fals, after 696 CE. Similar to Mattathias Antigonus prutah (37- 40 BCE).

#138
Jerusalem?, anonymous fals, after 696 CE. Similar to First Revolt shekel (66-70 CE).

Israel Coins Inspired by Ancient Judaean Coins

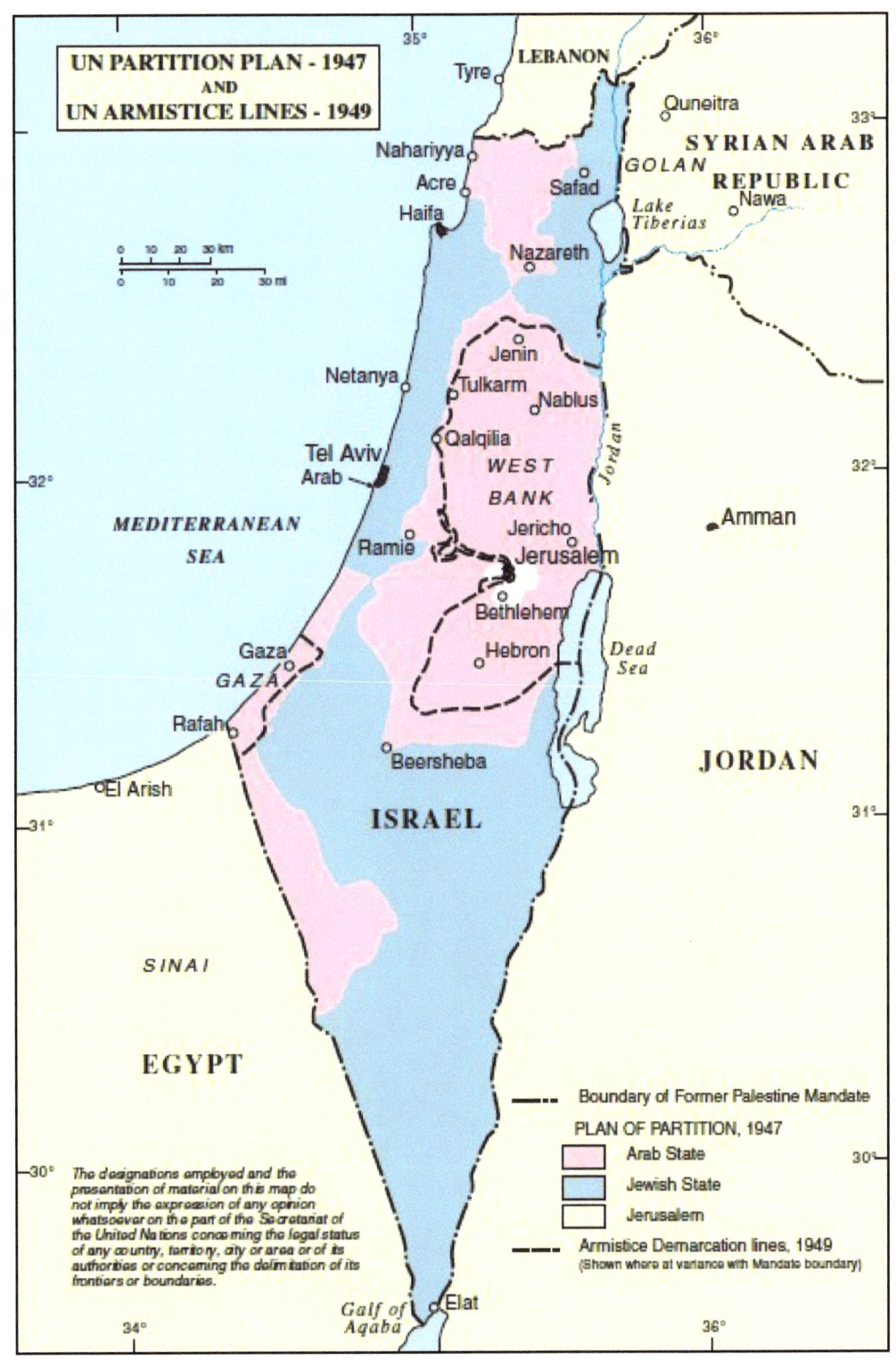

Fig. 46
Map of Israel, 1947-9, the period that its first coins were issued. Courtesy of the United Nations.

Mel Wacks

#139
Israel, 25 mils, issued 1948-9, and small bronze issued during the Second Revolt (132/133 CE).

#140
Israel, 1 prutah, issued in 1949, and prutah issued by Herod the Great (37–4 BCE).

#141
Israel, 5 prutot, issued in 1949, and medium bronze issued during the Second Revolt (132/133 CE).

#142
Israel, 10 prutot, issued in 1949, and large bronze issued during the Second Revolt (132/133 CE).

#143
Israel, 25 prutot, issued in 1949, and zuz issued during the Second Revolt (133/134 CE).

Soon after Israel's independence in 1948, the first coins in over 1,800 years were issued by a Jewish nation. According to Sylvia Haffner (*Israel's Modern Money and Medals 1917-1970*): "The new coins were designed with the object of reviving the ancient Jewish coins and their symbolic forms, and to create a link between the past of the Jewish people and the State of Israel."

#144
Israel, 50 prutot issued in 1949, and prutah issued during the First Revolt (67/68 CE).

#145
Israel, 250 prutot, issued in 1949, and quarter shekel issued during the First Revolt (69/70 CE).

#146
Israel, 500 prutot, issued in 1949, and shekel issued during the First Revolt (66-70 CE).

In 1960, Israel introduced coins denominated in units of agora and lira (pound). The designs again were inspired by ancient Judaean coins.

#147
Israel, 1 agora, issued 1960-1, and prutah issued by Herod Agrippa (42/43 CE).

#148
Israel, 10 agorot, issued 1960-77, and half [shekel], issued during the First Revolt (69/70 CE).

#149
Israel, 25 agorot, issued 1960-1979, and medium bronze issued during Second Revolt (134/135 CE).

#150
Israel, 1 lira (pound), issued 1967-80, and shekel issued during the First Revolt (66-70 CE).

And this tradition continued in Israel's later trade coins.

#151
Israel, 1 new sheqel, issued starting in 1985, featuring lily design from Yehud coin (4th century BCE).

#152
Israel, 2 sheqalim, issued starting in 2007, featuring double cornucopia design from Hasmonean coins (c. 135-37 BCE).

About the Author

Mel Wacks purchased his first ancient Judaean coin in 1963 — a Jewish Shekel — and his interest in this field blossomed, resulting in well over 100 published articles. First was "A New Comprehensive Method of Grading and Cataloging Ancient Coins," published in the July and August 1967 issues of *Numismatic Scrapbook Magazine*. In June of 1970, Mel published "Royal Symbol Discovered on Judaean Coin" in *The Numismatist*. His research on "Ezekial's Vision [on early Yehud Coin]" was prepared for the International Numismatic Congress in 1973, and was printed in *Spink's Numismatic Circular* in December, 1976. Mel's "The Jews, Jesus and the Jerusalem Temple Tax" was the lead article in the special Israel edition of *World Coins*, in July, 1975. Next was the publication of his *Handbook of Biblical Numismatics* in 1976 — leading to a series of over 100 "Biblical Byline" columns appearing in *World Coin News*.

Fig. 47
The above medal, celebrating Mel's 70th birthday, was created by Eugene Daub for the Jewish-American Hall of Fame in 2009.

Mel Wacks' most ambitious project was the launching of The Biblical Numismatic Society in 1977, in association with Ira Goldberg and Superior Coin Company. Membership reached 1,000 at the BNS's peak. Mel edited the BNS newsletter, *The Augur*, through 1983, publishing important articles by himself, as well as past and present scholars such as David Hendin, Prof. Baruch Kanael, Prof. Bruno Kisch, Leo Mildenberg, and A. Reifenberg, Ph.D. *The Augur* won the prestigious Best Club Publication Award from the Numismatic Literary Guild in 1979.

Mel Wacks, one of the founding board members of the American Israel Numismatic Association, has written numerous articles for its magazine, *The Shekel*, and was its editor from 2017 through 2020.

All issues of *The Shekel* and *The Augur* can be read on the Newman Numismatic Portal.

Last, but definitely not least, Mel Wacks has been Director of the Jewish-American Hall of Fame from its founding in 1969 through the present. He recently published the book *Medals of the Jewish-American Hall of Fame 1969-2019*.

Countless collectors have been motivated to specialize in ancient Judaean and related coins after reading *The Augur* or *The Handbook of Biblical Numismatics* — and Mel hopes that readers of his *Handbook of Bible Coins, 45th Anniversary Edition* will be similarly inspired.

Appendix A
Ancient Judaean Coin Inscriptions

Excerpts from "The Hebrew Coin Script: A Study in the Epigraphy of Ancient Jewish Coins"
By Leo Kadman
Originally published in *Israel Exploration Journal, Vol. 4, No. 3/4 (1954)*

Reifenberg, Narkiss, Mildenberg and many other scholars are united in the view that the script used on the Jewish coins was an artificial revival of the ancient Hebrew alphabet, some centuries after it had fallen into disuse. In Reifenberg's words: "one should therefore speak not of an epigraphic development, but only of an imitation of earlier forms."

However, especially in the light of the recently discovered Dead Sea Scrolls, David Diringer (in *Early Hebrew Writing*, The Biblical Archaeologist Vol. 13, No. 4, Dec. 1950), arrives at the conclusion "that it is hardly likely that an obsolete script would have been chosen for objects such as coins which are in general use and that it is highly probable that the early Hebrew writing survived until the second century of the Christian era and continued to be used among certain sections of the population for some centuries, after the Aramaic language and script had become the official means of intercourse."

It's satisfying to be able to read the ancient Hebrew coin inscriptions yourself — so there follows on the next pages, from left to right — paleo-Hebrew word on coin, equivalent English letters, English letters reversed (since Hebrew is read from right to left), transliteration, and English translation.

Samaria & Yehud	Hasmonean	Hasmonean Aramaic	First Revolt	Bar Kochba Revolt	English Transliteration (Sepharadi)	Modern Hebrew
	⌐	ᴧᴧ	⌐	⌐	(Holds vowel)	א
ㄩ	ㅋ		ㅋ	ㅋ	B	ב
	ᴧ	ᴧ	ㄱ	ㄱ	G	ג
ㄐㄐ	ㄐ	ㄱㄐ	ㄐ		D	ד
ㅋㄱ	ㅋㅋ	ᴨ	ㅋ	ㅋ	H	ה
Kᴧ	ĪĪĪ	ㄱ ㄑ	ㅏ	ㅏㅏㅏ	V/W/U	ו
ㅍ				ㅍ	Z	ז
日	日ロ		日	日	H	ח
					T	ט
ㅅㄹㄱ	ᴧㄹㄹ		ㄹ	ㄹ	Y	י
ㅅ	ㄱㄱㄱㄱ	ענככ		ㅋ	K/H	כ
ㄴ	ㄴㄴ	ㄴㄴㄴ	ㄴ	ㄴ	L	ל
ㅋ	ㅋㅋㅋ	ㅋㅋㅋ	ㅋ	ㅋ	M	מ
ㅋ	ㄴㄴㄴ	ㄴ	ㄴㄴ	ㄴㄴ	N	נ
◐		ㅇㅁ			S	ס
∪			○	○	(Holds vowel)	ע
ㅋ					P	פ
			ᴧㄹ		TZ	צ
ㄹ			ㅜㄹ		K	ק
ㅋ	ㅋ	ㄱㅋ	ㅋ	ㅋ	R	ר
ㅅ	ㅅㅅㅅ	ㅋ	w	w	S/Š	ש
ㄱ	ㅏㅅㅏ		×	×	T	ת

Fig. 48 Alphabets used on ancient Judaean coins.

Yehud Coins

𐤉𐤄𐤃	DHY	YHD	Yehud (the Judaean Province)

Hasmonean Coins

𐤉𐤄𐤅𐤇𐤍𐤍	NNHOHY	YHOHNN	Yehohanan (John Hyrcanus I, 135 - 104 BCE)
𐤉𐤄𐤅𐤃𐤄	HDOHY	YHODH	Yehudah (Judah Aristobulus I, 104 - 103 BCE)
𐤉𐤄𐤅𐤍𐤕𐤍	NTNOHY	YHONTN	Yehonatan (Alexander Jannaeus, 103 - 76 BCE)
𐤉𐤍𐤕𐤍𐤄	HNTNY	YNTNH	Yonatan (John Hyrcanus II, King 67 BCE, Ethnarch 63 - 40 BCE)
𐤌𐤕𐤕𐤉𐤄	HYTTM	MTTYH	Mattatayah (Mattathias Antigonus, 40 - 37 BCE)
𐤊𐤄𐤍	NHK	KHN	kohen – priest
𐤂𐤃𐤋	LDG	GDL	gadol - high
𐤓𐤀𐤔	ShOR	ROSh	rosh - head (of the council of the Jews, Hendin 1137 and 1138 only)
𐤇𐤁𐤓	RVH	HVR	chever - council (the Sanhedrin?)
𐤉𐤄𐤅𐤃𐤌	MYDOHY	YHODYM	Yehudim – [of the] Jews
𐤌𐤋𐤇	HLM	MLH	melech - king (on some Alexander Jannaeus coins)

First Revolt Coins

𐤉𐤔𐤓𐤀𐤋	LARSY	YSRAL	Yisrael – Israel (Year 1-5 Shekels & Half Shekels)
𐤔𐤒𐤋	LKSh	ShKL	shekel (Years 1-5 Shekels & Half Shekels)
𐤒𐤃𐤅𐤔𐤄	HShODK	KDOShH	kedusha – is holy (Year 1 Shekels & Half Shekels)
𐤄𐤒𐤃𐤅𐤔𐤄	HSh ODK	KDOShH	ha'kedusha – the holy (Year 2-5 Shekels & Half Shekels)
𐤉𐤓𐤅𐤔𐤋𐤌	MLShORY	YROShLM	Yeroshalam – Jerusalem (Year 1 Shekel & Half Shekel)

Script	Transliteration	Hebrew	Meaning
	MYLShORY	YROShLYM	Yeroshalayim – Jerusalem (Years 2-5 Shekels)
	TORḤ	ḤROT	charot – freedom (Years 2 & 3 Prutot)
	NOYTs	TsYON (Tsion)	Zion (Years 2 & 3 Prutot)
	TNSh	ShNT	shanat – year (Years 2 & 3 Prutot)
	MYTÅ	Å TYM	shtayim – two (Years 2 Prutah)
	SWLÅ	Å LWS	shalosh – three (Year 3 Prutah)
	TLAGL	LGALT	legulat – for the redemption (Year 4 Bronze Eighth?, Quarter & Half Shekels)
	ÕBRA	ARBÕ	arba – four (Year 4 Bronze Eighth?, Quarter & Half Shekels)
	YTsḤ	ḤTsY	chatsi – half (Years 1-5 Silver Half Shekels & Year 4 Bronze Half Shekel)
	ÕVR	RVÕ	reva – quarter (Years 1 & 4 Quarter Shekels and Year 4 Bronze Shekel)
		A[leph]	one (Year 1 Shekel and Half Shekel)
	B[et] Sh	Sh B[et]	Sh[anat] 2 – year 2 (Year 2 Shekel and Half Shekel)
	G[immel] Sh	Sh G[immel]	Sh[anat] 3 – year 3 (Year 3 Shekel and Half Shekel)
	D[alet] Sh	Sh D[alet]	Sh[anat] 4 – year 4 (Year 4 Shekel and Half Shekel)
	H[eh] Sh	Sh H[eh]	Sh[anat] 5 – year 5 (Year 5 Shekel and Half Shekel)

Second Revolt Coins

Script	Transliteration	Hebrew	Meaning
	MLShORY	YROShLM	Yeroshalam – Jerusalem (Year 1 Sela)
	NÕMSh	ShMÕN	Simon [Bar Kokhba]

Mel Wacks

שמעם	ÕMSh	ShMÕ	Sim[on Bar Kokhba] Also the first word in the Jewish Prayer: "Hear, O Israel: The Lord is our God; the Lord is one."
אלעזר	RZÕLA	ALÕZR	Elazar - Eleazar (Year 1)

Mildenberg observed that: "The two words 'Eleazar the Priest' never occur on the coins of the Bar Kokhba Rebellion in regular normal writing. The letters are grouped under the palm on the bronzes and around the jug on the denarii, in so many perplexing ways that generations of students had to make all kinds of efforts to decipher this legend. At first they thought [it was] even some secret code, in fact, a deliberate mystification" (*The Eleazar Coins of the Bar Kokhba Rebellion*, Historia Judaica 11, no.1, 1949, p. 80).

הכהן	NHCH	HCHN	HaCohen – the priest (Year 1)
נשיא	AYSN	NSYA	Nasi – leader (Middle Bronze)
שנת	TNSh	ShNT	shanat – year (Year 1 and 2)
אחת	TḤA	AḤT	echat – one (Year 1)
שב	B[et] Sh	Sh B[et]	Sh[enat] 2 - year 2 (Year 2)

Note: Ḥ is pronounced like the first Hebrew letter in Chanukah; Õ is an O-ish sounding vowel.

Bibliography: www.forumancientcoins.com

Appendix B
The Holy of Holies on Ancient Judaean Coins

Fig. 49
An unknown artist's engraving depicting the Holy of Holies.

Fig. 50
Second Revolt, (L to R) Year 1, Year 2 and Year 3 sela'im, 132-5 CE.

Let us examine possible origins of the various design elements on the sela, most of which are depicted on the above engraving. Keep in mind, that the Temple had been destroyed by the Romans at the conclusion of the First Revolt in 70 CE, so the image on the sela was a depiction of the Temple that Bar Kochba wanted to rebuild.

THE STAR above the temple on sela'im issued during the second year of the revolt could allude to the revolutionary leader Shim'on Bar Koseba, who was known as Bar Kochba, meaning "Son of the Star." This was in reference to messianic expectations of the verse: "There shall step forth a star [kochab] out of Jacob" (*Numbers 24:17*). Indeed, one of the greatest sages of the time — Rabbi Akiva — had proclaimed Bar Kochba as the messiah.

Mel Wacks 91

Fig. 51
Enlargements of Bar Kochba's "star" or Helena's "golden candelabra"?

On the other hand, this so-called "star" looks more like a sunburst of light on many of the coins — and that's one of the reasons why this may actually represent the golden candelabrum over the opening of the Temple sanctuary donated by Queen Helena in the early First Century CE, about half a century before the Beit Hamikdash (Temple at Jerusalem) was destroyed by the Romans, according to the Mishnah (m. *Yoma* 3:10). The Tosefta (*Yoma* 2:3) suggests that it not only had its own light, but early in the morning it reflected the sun's first rays. Thus, when the priests wanted to know whether it was already time to say the Shema prayer in the morning, they had only to look at Queen Helena's candelabrum.

Fig. 52
Helena's Golden Lamp. Courtesy of The Temple Institute.

Josephus in his *Antiquities of the Jews*, tells the story of Queen Helena of Adiabene (see Fig. 28 Map of the Armenian Kingdom) and her sons Kings Izates II and Monobazus II, and how they converted to Judaism in the mid-first century CE. According to Josephus, at a certain point during the reign of her son, Izates II (34-58 C.E.), after both had converted to Judaism, Helena decided to move to Judaea:

"Helena, the mother of the king, saw that peace prevailed in the kingdom and that her son [Izates II] was prosperous and the object of admiration in all men's eyes, even those of foreigners, thanks to the prudence God gave him. Now she had conceived a desire to go to the city of Jerusalem and to worship at the temple of God, which was famous throughout the world, and to make thank-offerings there" (*Ant. 20:49*).

According to Josephus, Helena returned to Adiabene in 58 CE, when her son Izates II died, and her other son, Monobazus II, took the throne. She must have been at least in her seventies at the time of this trip. Helena died soon after, and according to Josephus: "Monobazus [II] sent her bones and those of his brother [Izates II] to Jerusalem to be buried in the three pyramids that his mother had erected at a distance of three furlongs from the city of Jerusalem" (*Ant.* 20:94). The tomb of Helena and Izates is a large structure that still exists, but misidentified as "the Tomb of Kings."

THE WAVY LINE on some sela'im of the third year could represent an ornamental grape vine. *Mishnah Middot 3:8* indicates that "A golden vine stood at the door of the Sanctuary trained on poles, and anyone who offered a leaf or a grape or a bunch used to bring it and hang it there."

Fig. 53
Interestingly, a similar wavy line appeared, over 100 years earlier (while the Jerusalem Temple was still standing), above pagan temple columns on a coin of Herod Philip, 4 BCE-34 CE (H- -).

THE PILLARS: "And you shall place [dividing curtains] on four pillars of acacia wood, overlaid with gold" (*Exodus 26:32*).

THE BOX in the center could represent the Ark of the Covenant, containing the Ten Commandments: "They shall make an ark of acacia wood, two and a half cubits its length, a cubit and a half its width, and a cubit and a half its height" (*Exodus 25:10*).

THE STAFFS used to carry the Ark could be represented by the two dots within the box: "And you shall cast four golden rings for it, and you shall place them upon its four corners, two rings on its one side, and two rings on its other side. And you shall make poles of acacia wood and you shall overlay them with gold. And you shall bring the poles into the rings on the sides of the ark, to carry the ark with them" (*Exodus 25:12-14*).

THE ANGEL'S WINGS above the Ark could be represented on the sela'im by the the arch above the box: "And you shall make two golden cherubim; you shall make them of hammered work ... The cherubim shall have their wings spread upwards, shielding the ark cover with their wings" (*Exodus 25:18, 20*).

THE STEPS leading up to the Temple of Jerusalem (the horizontal ladder-like design under the columns) on sela'im of the second and third year could represent the 15 steps at the southern edge of Jerusalem's Temple Mount. Worshippers would enter the Temple from these steps: "Three times in the year, every one of your males shall appear before the Lord, your God, in the place He will choose: on the Festival of Matzoth and on the Festival of Weeks, and on the Festival of Sukkoth" (*Deuteronomy 16:16*). Some suggest the pilgrims sang Psalms 120-134 — each beginning with "A song of ascent" — as they climbed these steps. Ladder-like steps beneath a temple were also depicted on coins of Caesarea Maritima and others.

Fig. 54
Caesarea Maritima, with Trajan, 98-117 CE.

Two other important Jewish ceremonial objects, pictured in this engraving, appeared on an extremely rare prutah issued by Antigonus Mattathias in the last days of his reign (c. 40 BCE) — **THE MENORAH** and **TABLE OF SHEWBREAD**.

Fig. 55
Mattathias Antigonus, prutah, 40-37 BCE (H-1168).

And, finally, we come to objects contained *within* the Ark of the Covenant — the tablets containing the Ten Commandments, **THE GOLDEN POT OF MANNA**, and **AARON'S BUDDED ROD**. Of primary importance are the tablets containing the Ten Commandments: "And you shall place into the ark the testimony, which I will give you" (*Exodus 25:16*) — but these are not shown on any coin. However, the other two objects may have been portrayed on the shekels issued during the First Revolt.

Fig. 56
Fanciful picture of the Ark of the Covenant, containing the tablets of the Ten Commandments, the golden pot of manna and Aaron's budded rod.

Fig. 57
First Revolt, shekel, Year 3 = 68/69 CE (H-1361).

The Lubavitcher Rebbe, Rabbi Menachem M. Schneerson writes "The Rambam [includes in] the fourth chapter of Hilchos Beis HaBechirah … the following statement: **When [King Solomon] constructed the [Temple in Jerusalem] … Together with [the ark], were entombed Aaron's staff, the vial [of manna], and the anointing oil. All of these [sacred articles] did not return in the Second [Temple].** This is repeated in the New Testament, where *Hebrews 9:3-4* tells how **"The tabernacle which is called the Holiest of all … wherein was the golden pot that had manna, and Aaron's rod that budded."** Furthermore, "[Aaron's rod] put forth buds, produced blossoms, and bore ripe almonds" (*Numbers 17:8*).

Fig. 58
Young almonds crowned with dried petals — resembling the motif on the shekels.
Photo from "Nature and Landscape in Jewish Heritage" by Noga HaReuveny.

Hendin (*Guide to Biblical Coins*) calls these motifs a "ritual chalice" and "pomegranate buds," Meshorer (*Jewish Coins of the Second Temple Period*) describes them as a "chalice" and "stem with three fruit pomegranates," Madden (*Coins of the Jews*) calls them "a cup or chalice" and "?Aaron's rod." Pot of manna or chalice, Aaron's rod of almond buds or three pomegranates, or somethings else — take your choice.

Appendix C
The Roman Tenth Legion

Legio X Fretensis was a legion of the Imperial Roman army. It was founded by the young Gaius Octavius (later to become Augustus Caesar) in 41/40 BCE to fight during the period of civil war that started the dissolution of the Roman Republic.

In 66 CE, Legion X Fretensis moved to Judaea to suppress the revolt. In 68, the Xth destroyed the monastery of Qumran, where the Dead Sea Scrolls originated. In 70, the Xth camped on the Mount of Olives and used war machines to hurl 25 kg stones 400 meters at the ramparts of besieged Jerusalem. After a five-month siege and the horrors of starvation, the city was taken and then completely destroyed. In 73 CE, after a long siege, the Xth — along with auxiliary troops and thousands of Jewish prisoners — broke through the fortification wall atop Masada, the last Jewish stronghold. The Jewish defenders chose mass suicide before the final assault. After the revolt, the Xth was the sole legion in Judaea, garrisoned at Jerusalem. Legion X Fretensis is recorded to have existed at least until 410 CE.

X Fretensis symbols were the bull — the holy animal of the goddess Venus (mythical ancestor of the gens Julia) — a ship (probably a reference to the Battles of Naulochus and/or Actium), the god Neptune, and a boar. The bull — zodiac symbol of Taurus — may also mean that this Legion was organized between April 20th and May 20th.

Roman countermarks did not come into use until the introduction of the imperial era by Augustus. Possible reasons have been proposed by Richard Baker, in a talk to the Ancient Coin Club of Los Angeles, as to why a coin might be countermarked:
(1) To extend the geographical area in which the coin would be accepted as legal tender.
(2) To extend the life of a coin which had been in circulation for a considerable period of time.
(3) To designate a new authority usurping the coins of another for their own use.

All of these reasons probably account for the numerous Judaean coins found with counterstamps of the Roman Tenth Legion Fretensis – LEG X or a galley ship. Each counterstamped coin is unique, and most are of very low quality (per reason #2). Here are some examples:

Fig. 59
Well worn coin with countermarks of a galley and "L•X•F" (Legion X Fretensis) above a boar standing over a dolphin. Issued for reasons #2 and #3.

Fig. 60
Ascalon, time of Vespasian and Titus (69-81 CE). "X" countermark over bust of Tyche. Probably created for reasons #1 and 2.

Fig. 61

Fourth Year of the First Revolt (69/70 CE) [1/8th Shekel?] with clear countermarks "LXF" and a boar. Issued for reason #3.

Fig. 62

Second Revolt, "Eleazar Hakohen," small denomination, Year 1 = 132/133 C.E. With galley countermark, representing Legion X Fretensis. Issued for reason #3.

After the Temple fell in 70 CE, the Tenth Legion began its own building program for its garrison. It made tiles for both its roof and floors in several areas, like baths.

Fig. 63

This floor tile even has some of the original mortar on it. The stamp reads "LEG X FR" and is within an incused rectangle. Source: www.legionten.org, from the collection of Terry Nix.

Fig. 64

This limestone inscription comes from Jerusalem or Samaria and belongs to the first or second century CE The inscription reads "LEG X FRE COH IIX" (10th Legion, 8th cohort) and it is decorated with dolphins and a wild boar, symbols of the legion. Photo © The Israel Museum, Jerusalem.

Mel Wacks 97

Appendix D
About Ira Goldberg

This article was originally published in 1982 in *The Augur*.
Ira Goldberg is currently co-owner of Ira & Larry Goldberg Auctioneers.

Fig. 65
Ira Goldberg purchased antiquities from Moshe Dayan, the great Israeli hero and collector of ancient Judaica.

For the past dozen years I have averaged two or three trips to the Holy Land, always in pursuit of biblical and ancient coins. The bronze coins have always been scarce, especially in choice condition. They were scarce ten years ago, and are even more scarce today. This is not true with the silver coins. During my first trip, which was after the 1967 Yom Kippur War, a lot of bronze pieces entered the market place. This was due primarily to the tilling of the land in the expanded territories acquired by Israel as a result of the war.

Most of the coins are found by the Bedouins, who have a well organized network. The nomadic Bedouin tribes are broken down to various areas. Certain Bedouins are in charge of jewelry finds, others are in charge of coin finds. These coins initially find their way into the Damascus market place, Jerusalem, Lebanon and various other ports. The Bedouins, because they speak the same Arab languages, feel closer with the other Arabs in the region, and have been able to do business with them for centuries. Thus, the original source for most ancient Jewish coins are Arab merchants.

In my trips to this part of the world, I have dealt directly with the Bedouin headmasters. Many times I have waited while the Bedouins come in, three or four together, and have bought coins within hours of them having come out of the ground! I remember one clump I saw in 1968 when I was in my early twenties on my first trip to Israel. It was done in a very clandestine manner, late at night. I was scared half to death. I was offered a group of Bar Kochba tetradrachms at $600 a piece. I didn't even know if the coins were genuine or not. I said I would buy four and they proceeded to actually take a chisel and knock a piece of the clump away and we figured that was four coins. After I got back to the U.S., I put the coins in sulphuric acid. There were four tetradrachms and three or four denarii in between. I went back six months later and of course the hoard had been completely dispersed.

Fig. 66
Ira Goldberg saw "clumps" of coins — that probably looked
something like this clump of Shekels found at Masada.

Silver coins — the shekels of the First Revolt, the Bar Kochba tetradrachms and denarii — have always been reasonably plentiful. The prices of these coins have remained fairly steady for the past dozen years due to the hoards that have been found. On each of my trips to Israel I always saw "fresh" pieces. I would probably see at least three or four different groups of shekels numbering anywhere from ten pieces at a time; on my last trip I saw a total of 171 shekels! The tetradrachms are never quite as prevalent as the shekels. As of the last couple years, the shekels are about $1000 a piece when bought in quantity from Arab sources; the denarii are two or three hundred dollars a piece. Once in a while you will find a rare variety in the wholesale lots, one that is retrograde or one that has been struck a little differently, but most of these merchants, Arabs and Bedouins, are no dummies. They all have Meshorer catalogs, Reifenberg's book, and they know the common coins from the scarce ones. They know a dated tetradrachm from an undated one, or a dated denarius from an undated denarius, and they know a rare year one shekel from a two year or three.

Back in the late 1960's and early 1970's, it was possible to see a hoard of shekels, year two's and three's, or more rarely (perhaps 10%) you would find a year one at a good price. However, this is no longer the case. Also, a dozen years ago you would see half shekels. I don't believe I have seen a half shekel hoard in the last five years. The half shekels are truly very scarce coins, and when found, they never seem to be in the state of preservation of the shekels. They are always in a lower more circulated condition. This proves to me that they must have been struck in far smaller quantities than the shekels.

On the last three or four trips I made to Israel I found it increasingly difficult to buy any Jewish silver coins! I firmly believe that these sources are drying up. The land has been tilled and it is far more unlikely that any large new hoards will be found.

When dealing with the Arab merchants, you have to put a price on the material. Everything is sold in groups. For example, if you are looking at a hoard of shekels, you cannot ask what they want for it. You have to make an offer and they will contact you later. They have to talk to their counterparts or whoever else they have to advise, because the one merchant may be representing six or seven different people on a find. They contact you, the price always had to be negotiated and you never really know that you have a deal until the coins are actually in your hands. There were many times where we agreed on a price and the coins were never delivered to me as agreed upon. I would get a phone call or a telegram, make a trip to Israel, and the coins were nothing like they were described to me. So you never really know what you are getting until the transaction is completed. At times, this can be a very frustrating experience. What will happen is you will see a group, like the 171 shekels I saw. I viewed them and made my offer which I believe was $900 a coin. Twenty percent of the hoard was probably superb EF's, 20% had chisel marks with faults, and maybe 60% of the hoard would cleanup to be VF-EF. With all the coins uncleaned, you had to take a chance when you bought a hoard like this. There were no year one shekels, only year two's. I saw this hoard and they told me they would advise me. In three days a merchant contacted me and I saw about thirty coins, definitely from the same hoard with the same toning. Another day I was shown twenty-two pieces, definitely from the same hoard. The competing Arab dealers would try to con each other out of the sale or try to get a higher price from me, I was never quite sure. The result was that I never was able to buy one coin from the hoard! I have been back twice since and was told that a German coin dealer purchased the entire hoard and he then sold them to a museum intact. I cannot confirm this, but I do know the coins are no longer on the Israeli market. I have numerous contacts in major cities in Israel, as well as throughout Europe, who are on the lookout for Jewish coins. Nothing new has come to light. There have been no new recent hoards.

For the past dozen or so years I have probably sold more shekels, tetradrachms and silver denarii than virtually anyone else in the coin business. I personally must have handled 250 to 300 shekels and maybe 100 to 150 tetradrachms, and have seen hundreds more. Of all the tetradrachms I have handled, less than 1% or 2% are coins that I would call superb. If you can find tetradrachms that are completely struck with all lettering clear and sharp, well centered, I think they are an especially good buy. And this is true with the overstruck denarii as well. If you can get a silver denarius that has full lettering and is well struck or shows some of the underlying coin, I think these are the coins to buy.

Appendix E
Estimated Coin Values
Prepared by Ira Goldberg

Note that estimated retail values are indicated for bronze coins with grades averaging Very Fine, and for silver coins with grades averaging Extremely Fine. Actual prices will vary due to many factors, including strike, centering, surfaces, wear, and eye appeal.

#	Value	#	Value	#	Value	#	Value	#	Value
1	$3,000	29	$75	57	$250	85	$7,500	113	$1,500
2	$250	30	$200	58	$75	86	$7,000	114	$1,000
3	$1,000	31	$250	59	$75	87	$750	115	$5,000
4	$1,300	32	$225	60	$75	88	$1,000	116	$5,000
5	$2,000	33	$200	61	$150	89	$600	117	$500
6	$5,000	34	$750	62	$125	90	$1,000	118	$500
7	$2,500	35	$100	63	$125	91	$30,000	119	$500
8	$2,500	36	$150	64	$100	92	$30,000	120	$500
9	RRR	37	$300	65	$100	93	$30,000	121	$300
10	$75	38	$650	66	$75	94	$15,000	122	$300
11	$7,500	39	$750	67	$400	95	$1,000	123	$300
12	$75	40	$2,000	68	RRR	96	$3,500	124	$400
13	$75	41	$70	69	$12,500	97	$300	125	$400
14	$75	42	$3,500	70	$17,500	98	$1,500	126	$75,000
15	$50	43	$50,000	71	$500,000	99	$300	127	$600
16	$250	44	$600	72	$6,000	100	$350	128	$400
17	$50	45	$500	73	$12,500	101	$400	129	$1,000
18	$50	46	$1,000	74	$6,000	102	$7,500	130	$800
19	$30	47	$1,000	75	$12,500	103	$250	131	$2,000
20	$100	48	$60	76	$25,000	104	$4,500	132	$18,000
21	$75	49	$60	77	$300,000	105	$30,000	133	$18,000
22	$900	50	$60	78	RRR	106	$20,000	134	$18,000
23	$675	51	$60	79	$50,000	107	$1,000	135	$10,000
24	$75,000	52	$80	80	RRR	108	$10,000	136	$100
25	$500	53	$80	81	$150	109	$6,000	137	$100
26	$500	54	$75	82	$150	110	$5,000	138	$100
27	$500	55	$125	83	$300	111	$6,000		
28	RRR	56	$250	84	$3,500	112	$2,500		

Appendix F
False Shekels

Fig. 67
Engraving of Gorlitz, 1580.

All of the False Shekels made for over 500 years are evidently a result of a pilgrimage made to the Holy Land by Georg Emerich (1422-1507), burgomaster of Gorlitz in Germany. When Emerich returned to his home town he had a reproduction of the Holy Sepulcher built. He distributed silver shekel tokens to those who visited his shrine, and these became the model for all other so-called False Shekels.

It is obvious that the designer of the False Shekels had not seen a real ancient shekel. He also could not have seen a picture of an ancient shekel, since the first illustration did not appear until 1538. So he must have relied on written descriptions — such as made by the great rabbi Moses ben Nahman (Nachmanides), in 1268: "The Lord has blessed me so greatly, for I have been so fortunate as to come to Acco and there to find in the hands of the elders of the land a silver coin with engravings, on one side resembling the branch of an almond tree, one the other some sort of dish … [The Samaritans] say that the shapes are Aaron's staff, with its almonds and blossoms, and the other shape, the container of manna."

The original Gorlitz chalice, overflowing with manna, was transformed on later False Shekels into a smoking censer, perhaps based on this biblical passage: "[The High Priest] shall place the ketoret (a special blend of eleven herbs and balms) upon the fire before God; and the cloud of the incense shall envelop the covering of the [Ark of] Testimony" (*Leviticus 16:13*).

The reverse of the False Shekel appears to have been inspired by: "And on the following day Moses came to the Tent of Testimony, and behold, Aaron's staff for the house of Levi had blossomed! It gave forth blossoms, sprouted buds, and produced ripe almonds" (*Numbers 17:23*).

Fig. 68
Early "Gorlitz-style" False Shekel.

Fig. 69
Nineteenth century False Shekel (R) with original box of issue (L).

Appendix G
Enlarged Photos of Small Coins

In order to show the design details, pictures of coins 20mm or smaller have been enlarged by 50% (1.5x), 16mm or smaller have been enlarged by 100% (2x), and coins 10mm or smaller have been enlarged by 200% (3x), as follows:

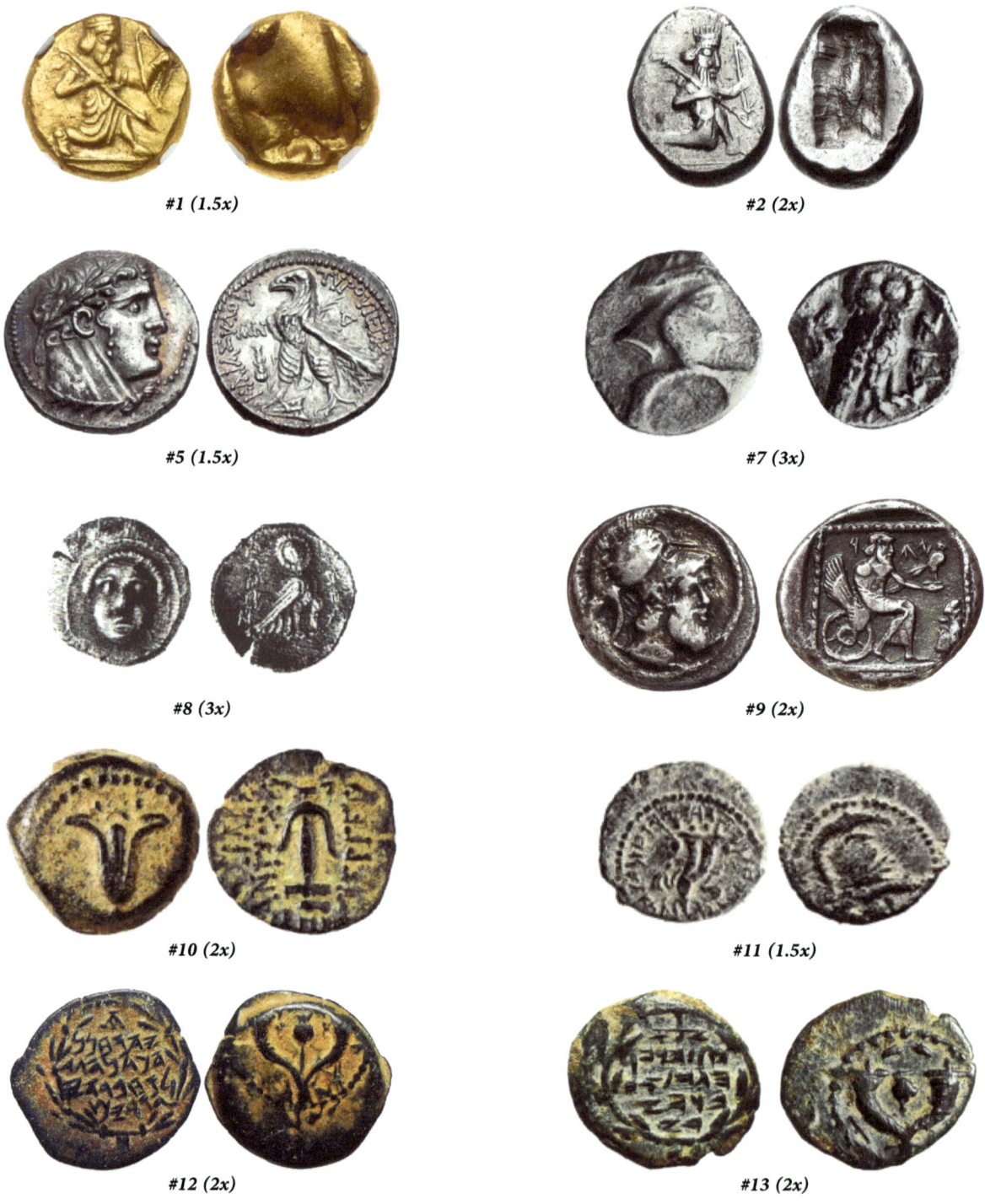

#1 (1.5x)   *#2 (2x)*

#5 (1.5x)   *#7 (3x)*

#8 (3x)   *#9 (2x)*

#10 (2x)   *#11 (1.5x)*

#12 (2x)   *#13 (2x)*

104 The Handbook of Biblical Numismatics

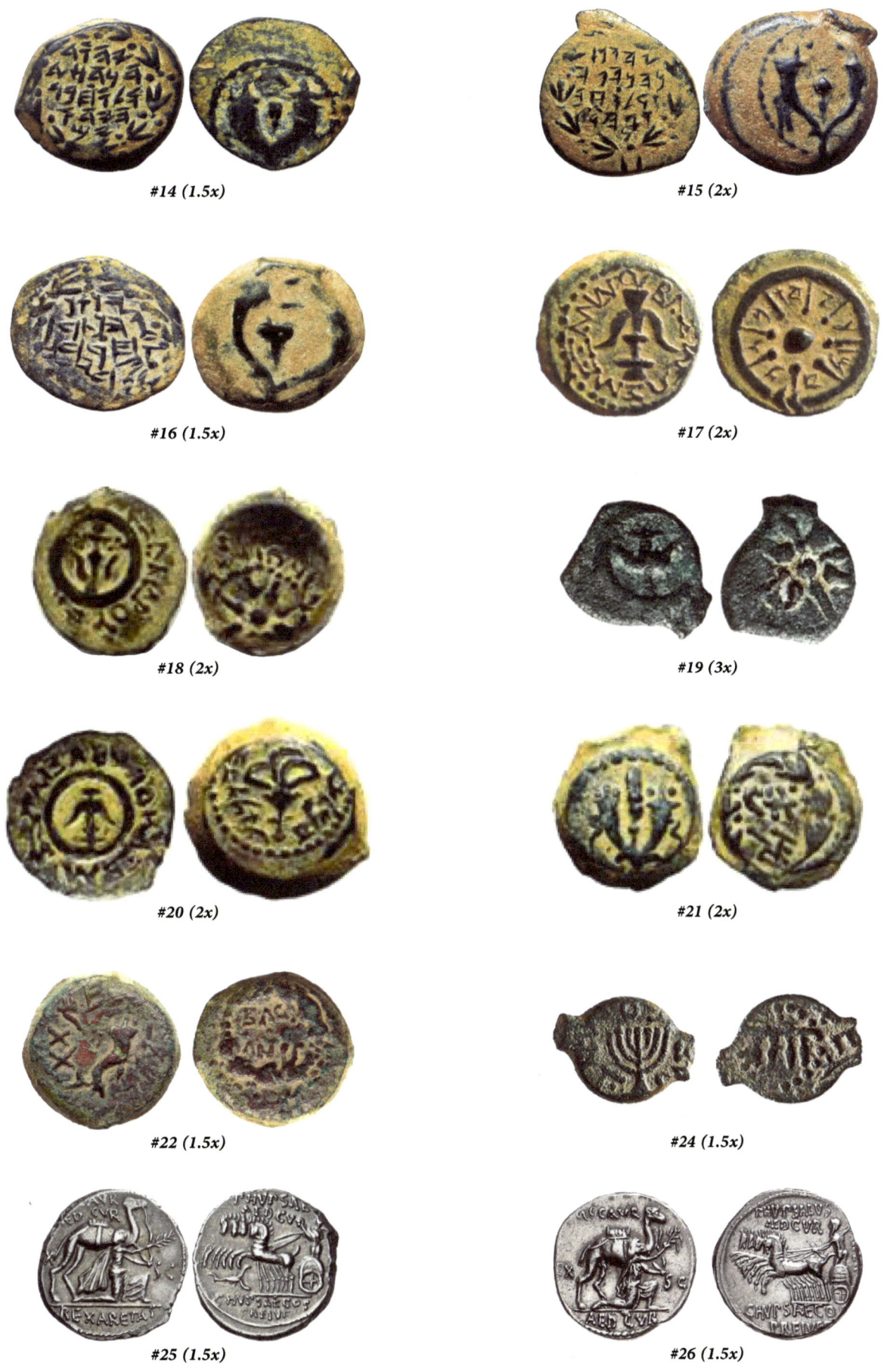

#14 (1.5x)

#15 (2x)

#16 (1.5x)

#17 (2x)

#18 (2x)

#19 (3x)

#20 (2x)

#21 (2x)

#22 (1.5x)

#24 (1.5x)

#25 (1.5x)

#26 (1.5x)

#27 (1.5x)

#28 (1.5x)

#29 (2x)

#30 (2x)

#31 (1.5x)

#32 (1.5x)

#33 (1.5x)

#35 (2x)

#36 (2x)

#37 (1.5x)

#39 (1.5x)

#40 (3x)

106   The Handbook of Biblical Numismatics

#41 (2x)

#43 (1.5x)

#46 (2x)

#47 (2x)

#48 (2x)

#49 (2x)

#50 (2x)

#51 (2x)

#52 (2x)

#53 (2x)

#54 (2x)

#55 (2x)

Mel Wacks 107

#70 (1.5x) #71 (2x)

#73 (1.5x) #75 (1.5x)

#77 (1.5x) #78 (1.5x)

#80 (1.5x) #81 (2x)

#82 (2x) #83 (1.5x)

#87 (1.5x) #88 (1.5x)

Mel Wacks

#125 (1.5x) #136 (1.5x)

#137 (1.5x) #138 (1.5x)

Appendix H
Poppies or Pomegranates?

This additional information was added shortly before publication.

Most of the small bronze prutot issued by the Hasmoneans feature a tiny round plant in between double cornucopia (horns of plenty). The plant has been described as a *poppy* by Madden (1864) and Reifenberg (1940); and as a *pomegranate* by De Saulcy (1854), Romanoff (1944), Meshorer (1967), Hendin (2010), and Shoshana Collection (2012).

Poppy proponents have this to say: "The poppy, as an Augustan emblem of peace and fertility, was 'exported' outside of Rome" (*Visual Representations of the Poppy in Greek and Roman Art*, Dr. Rivka Gersht). According to Meshorer (*Ancient Jewish Coinage*), there had existed at Samaria-Sebaste, prior to Herod's time, a cult of growth and fertility centered on worship of the Greek goddess Demeter … whose characteristic attributes were ears of wheat and poppy capsules. Herod is known to have erected a temple to Augustus at Samaria-Sebaste and is believed to have "depicted the poppy on his coinage to honor the local cult of Demeter and Kore at Samaria" (*Highs and Lows in The Holy Land: Opium in Biblical Times*, Eretz-Israel: Archaeological, Historical and Geographical Studies, Yigael Yadin Memorial Volume, Robert S. Merrillees). Dr. Nicholas Mittica Jr. goes one step further and proposes that "Herod the Great was perhaps the greatest of the middlemen in the opium supply to the Roman Empire" (*Herod the Great and the Roman Opium Trade*, www.romaneclipse.com).

Pomegranate advocate Romanoff (*Jewish Symbols on Ancient Jewish Coins*) writes "The pomegranate … had early assumed the meaning of blessing and fertility. It also connoted piety [and] good deeds." Also, "[Pomegranates] won a place among the symbol-plants that were employed in the Temple of Jerusalem … on each of the two columns … which stood at the entrance to the sanctuary … and pomegranates were suspended from [the high priest's] mantle."

The plant buds on the Hasmonean coins are usually crude, but are clear on some coins. A minority of these Hasmonean coins even show tiny bunches of grapes dangling from the cornucopia.

Fig. 70
Hasmonean prutot, c. 135-40 BCE. (L) Bud with prominent ridges.
(M) & (R) Relatively smooth buds, with tiny bunches of grapes hanging from cornucopia. Photos enlarged.

What is most obvious, is that the bud is atop a long thin stem. Secondly, the bud is not smooth — but has ridges — exactly like poppy buds. Since the bulbous green fruit of the poppy plant yields opium, it was used as a painkiller and hypnotic drug by the ancient Jews. The *Jerusalem Talmud* (TJ, Av. Zar. 2:2, 40d), c. 200 CE, gives a warning against using opium in the form of eye salves.

Fig. 71
(L) Poppy plants. (R) Drawing of poppy bud, Kohler's Medizinal-Pflanzen, 1887.

On the other hand, pomegranate buds are smooth with large pointed crowns, and they grow on short stems upside down in bunches:

Fig. 72
Pomegranate buds.

Further evidence that the object in between the cornucopia is a poppy, is that poppies are associated with cornucopia on other coins. For instance, "as a symbol of abundance, in Hellenistic and Roman works of art, the poppy was included within the content of the horn of plenty on the silver decadrachm of Queen Arsinoe II" (*Visual Representations of the Poppy in Greek and Roman Art*, Dr. Rivka Gersht), minted in nearby Egypt.

Fig. 73
Egypt, Queen Arsinoe II, decadrachm, 270 BCE. With large poppy atop cornucopia, and hanging bunches of grapes. Photo enlarged.

Herod the Great followed the Hasmonean rulers of Judaea. He also issued small bronze prutot with double cornucopia — but the budding plant within was replaced by a heathen symbol — a caduceus.

Fig. 74
Herod the Great, 2 prutot, 37 BCE. Photo enlarged.

A 2 prutot coin was issued by Herod featuring a plant that, since the mid-19th century, most expert numismatists have identified as a pomegranate. However, in 1982 Meshorer (*Ancient Jewish Coinage*) wrote: "In order to determine which of these two interpretations is correct, we collected casts and photographs of the best preserved coins depicting this design, and presented them to several botanists for analysis. All agreed that the design was a poppy. It depicts the three characteristics of this plant: a knob below the bottom, a wide calyx, and a flat bottom and top. Conversely, the pomegranate lacks the knob, and has a smaller and sometimes taller calyx; it also has a round shape." QED.

Index

Aaron's Rod 52-53, 102
Abraham 8
Abu Jara 69
Adventvi Avg Ivdaeae 65
Aelia Capitolina 74
Akiva (Rabbi) 91
Akko 11, 75
Alexander the Great 10
Alexandra, Salome 21
Ambibulus 44
Antiochus VII 17
Antigonus, Mattathias 23, 31
Antipater 33
Antony, Mark 31
Apameia 76
Aretas III 28
Armenia 42-43
Aristobulus, Judah 21
Aristobulus of Chalcis 40
Ascalon 73

Bacchus 29
Bachius Judaeus 29
Bar Kochba, Shim'on 67

Caesarea 74
Cleopatra VII 73
Common Era (CE) 7
Coponius 44

Daric 9
Deutsch, Robert 52

Eleazar the Priest 67
Esther 9
Ezekial 16

Felix, Antonius 47

Festus, Gessius 47
First Revolt 50-55
Fiscus Judaicus 60

Gamla 54
Goldberg, Ira 98-101
Gorlitz 102
Gratus, Valerius 45

Hacksilber 8
Hadrian, Publius Aelius 65-66
Hasmoneans 20
Helena (Queen) 92
Hendin, David 51, 52-53, 58-59, 67
Herod of Chalcis 40
Herod the Great 31, 34-35
Herod Agrippa I 40
Herod Agrippa II 40, 47
Herod Antipas 37
Herod Archelaus 37
Herod Philip II 38
Hezekiah 16
Holly of Hollies 91
Hyrcanus, John 20

Isaiah 57
Islamic Coins 80

Jannaeus, Alexander 21
Jerusalem 14, 18
Josephus 10, 16, 30, 32, 47, 51, 76
Judaea 13
Judaea Capta 56-59

Kadman, Leo 65
Kitos War 62

Lulav & Etrog 53-54, 68
Maccabees 10, 17, 18, 29
Madden, Frederic 52,
Maimonides (Rambam) 53, 95
Manna 52-53, 94-95
Menorah 23, 24
Meshorer, Ya'akov 14, 21, 47
Mishnah 40, 71
Mite 26
Moses 8
Moses ben Nahman (Rabbi) 102

Nabataea 28
Nachmanides 53
Neapolis 74, 78
Nerva, Marcus 60
New Testament 13, 14, 25, 34, 37, 40, 41, 46, 47, 48
Noah 77

Omar (Khalif) 80
Omer 52

Paul 47
Philo of Alexandria 46
Pilate, Pontius 46
Plautius, Aulus 29, 30
Pomegranates 21, 52, 112-114
Poppies 21, 112-114
Prutah 18

Quietus, Lusius 62

Romanoff, Paul 52

Salome 40

Scaurus, Marcus Aemilius   28
Schneerson, Menachem
    (Rebbe)   95
Second Revolt   66-71
Sela   67
Sepphoris   74
Suetonius   60
Shekel of Israel   51
Siglos   9
Sofaer, Abraham   Back cover
Sosius, Gaius   31
Syria   17

Tacitus   30
Talmud   67, 71
Temple Tax   13
Tiberias   37
Tiberius Caesar Augustus   49
Tigranes V   42
Tigranes VI   43
Torah (Old Testament)   9, 13,
    16, 34, 44, 52, 57, 68, 77,
    91, 94, 102
Trajan, Marcus Ulpius   62-63
Tribute Penny   48-49
Tyre   11

Vespasian, Titus Flavius   57

Wacks, Mel   85, Back Cover
Widow's Mite   25

Yahweh   16
Yehud   14, 16

Zabinas, Alexander   21
Zuz   68

Picture Credits

Every effort has been made by the author to reproduce photos of the finest coin specimens available at auction or on the Internet. Some of these photos have been found on the following websites:

American Numismatic Society: www.numismatics.org

Australian Numismatic Society www.the-ans.com

Marc Breitsprecher Coins: www.mrbcoins.com

The British Museum: www.britishmuseum.org

Goldberg Auctions: www.goldbergcoins.com

Classic Numismatic Group: www.cngcoins.com

Fontanille Coins: www.fontanillecoins.com

Forum Ancient Coins: www.forumancientcoins.com

Heritage Auctions: www.ha.com

The Israel Museum: www.imj.org.il

Fritz Rudolf Künker GmbH & Co. KG, Osnabrück: www.kuenker.de

Münzkabinett der Staatlichen Museen zu Berlin: www.smb.museum

Nomos nomosag.com

Numismatics Ars Classica www.arsclassicacoins.com

Numismatic Guaranty Corporation www.ngccoin.com

Shekel, The Online Catalog of Israel Numismatics: www.sheqel.info

Vcoins, the Online Coin Show: www.Vcoins.com

Wildwinds www.wildwinds.com

Zurqieh Dubai L.L.C

Zuzim Coins: www.zuzimcoins.com

You are invited to visit

www.amuseum.org